NORFOLK VICAR

The Curious Conduct of Curates & Clergymen

Tom Hughes

HALSGROVE

First published in Great Britain in 2009

Copyright © Tom Hughes 2009

British Library Cataloguing-in-Publication Data
A CIP record for this title is available from the British Library

ISBN 978 1 84114 862 5

HALSGROVE
Halsgrove House,
Ryelands Industrial Estate,
Bagley Road, Wellington, Somerset TA21 9PZ
Tel: 01823 653777   Fax: 01823 216796
email: sales@halsgrove.com

Part of the Halsgrove group of companies
Information on all Halsgrove titles is available at: www.halsgrove.com

Printed and bound by Shortrun Press, Exeter

Contents

Introduction

A really good clerical scandal, well-spiced and judiciously prolonged …
is worth fifty pounds a week to The Times.
The Churchman's Family Magazine (1863)

No one who examines the great bulk of Victorian clergymen of the Church of England can fail to remark upon their overwhelming piety and propriety; their zeal for their church and their faithful; and their selfless devotion to their calling amidst varying and often quite trying circumstances. Happily, their stories have been reverently celebrated elsewhere or, perhaps, their overdue recognition shall not come in this temporal world.

In this series, however, we recall the clergymen who featured in the numerous clerical scandals of the old Queen's long reign. Let me cede to others the deep and often bitter history of tithe wars, rows over reredos and rubric, churchyard and schoolroom; squabbles that very often became personal and quite nasty. Instead, we relate the stories of those clergymen whose personal life or family life - be they innocent or guilty – would become the subject of scandal and gossip. Adulterers, cads, and cuckolds were found in villages, market towns and even in the cathedral close. As one weary Archbishop declared, "You have certain scandals, not arising frequently, but from time to time, and echoed all round the sky until it seems as if the air was full of them." These are the stories from the county of Norfolk.

ACKNOWLEDGEMENTS

The staff at the British Library, St. Pancras & Colindale: The Lambeth Palace Library and The National Archives, Kew. The editors of Crockford's Clerical Directory. In the USA: The Library of Congress in Washington, DC; the Woodruff Library, Emory University, Atlanta, GA; and the Sterling Memorial Library, Yale University, New Haven CT, USA. I must also thank individually – and most especially, Wendy Sterry & Eve McClure, The Norfolk & Norwich Millenium Library and the Rev. Jess Stubenbord, of Mulbarton Rectory, in Norfolk. Additionally, I thank Lisa Brown, the Boston Library, Lincolnshire; Philip Duke, Berridge family genealogist; Paul Everest, The Library, St John's College, Cambridge; Clare Sexton, Lambeth Palace Library and Eddie Smith, Archivist at Westminster School.

I am extremely grateful for the opportunity and counsel I have received from Simon Butler of Halsgrove Publishing. Finally, I thank my wife, Kathleen McGraw, for all the reasons she knows, and certainly not limited to her excellent proofreading and faultless chauffeuring.

Go, Before I Chop Your Head Off!

The Rev. A.W. Bailey, curate of Outwell

Against scandal the minister is the most defenseless man in the community because, like Caesar's wife, he must be absolutely above suspicion; and there is no one the community suspects with more zest. Almost any woman's word will be believed against his own; and the newspapers are greedy for any scandal in which a minister is involved. This makes him a shining mark for a blackmailer.

McClure's Magazine (March 1914)

IN THOSE last months before the Great War, the Rev. Arthur Wellesley Bailey was a curate at London's famous Church of St. Martin's-in-the-Field. If he happened across the above article in his secular reading, no doubt a grim smile passed his lips. For in 1898, while a clergyman in the Norfolk fens he had claimed to be a victim of just such a plot.

Bailey began his clerical career far from Norfolk and London. He was born in Oxford in 1853 and had been educated at the Christian Missionary College in Islington. Founded in 1825, the college offered a "sound education in theology, science and classical learning" before sending its graduates out to preach among the heathen peoples of the world. Bailey went forth to India where he was ordained in the Church of England at Lahore in 1879. He spent nearly a full decade on the Afghan-Himalayan frontier. In 1884, he was mentioned as being in the remote village of Kotgurh, at 6600 feet, on the high road from Simla to Thibet. It was a place of seasonal weather extremes. The annual sacrifice of a village maiden had only recently been suppressed. The historian of those distant missions conceded that the young Rev. Bailey "has had many trials in his solitary position." In 1889, he left the mountain missions behind and returned to England.

In many ways, resuming his clerical career at home, he was still leading a form of nomadic existence. As a curate, he moved every two years, from Hertford to Thorpe Hamlet to London's Belsize Park. In 1897, now in his early forties, he arrived at the fens village of Outwell, near Wisbech. Well Creek, a branch of the Nene, creates a twisted border between Norfolk and Cambridgeshire. The village of Outwell straddles that border but the church of St. Clement's stands and most of the residents live on the Norfolk side. Mr. Bailey had come there to be a six-month *locum tenens* in the place of the absent rector, the Rev. Henry Venn Ellis. In late April of 1898, the Rev. Mr. Ellis' return was imminent and the Rev. Mr. Bailey had to leave the rectory and find other lodgings. He approached a local tenant farmer by the name of John Robb.

Born in the nearby village of Emneth, John Robb was just 23 and a newlywed, his wife Mary Ann, from Outwell, was only 18. The Robbs were parishioners and Mary had assisted with the Sunday school program. Though John and Mary Ann had been married only the previous November, not six months previously, they had an infant son. This was hardly unusual. John Robb and the Rev. Bailey agreed that the clergyman would have a sitting room on the ground floor and a bedroom on the first floor. He would pay ten shillings a week for the room and an additional fifteen shillings for meals. With all his belongings, Bailey came to the Robbs' farm on the night of 30 April 1898. Only a fortnight later, Bailey was forced to make a sudden departure. John Robb charged that the clergyman had made repeated attempts to seduce his young wife. Mr. Bailey, of course, insistently denied it and counterclaimed that he was the victim of a desperate blackmailer. Who was to be believed?

On Saturday, the 4th of June, the Wisbech magistrates gathered to hear what *The Eastern Daily Press* had promptly headlined: "Charge Against a Clergyman: Allegations by His Landlady." The hearing room was crowded as "Outwell and Upwell people were early on the scene." Mary Ann Robb was the first witness. We have no description of Mary Ann. However, an 18th Century visitor to Outwell, Lord Orford, wrote in his diary, "Women very ugly." We shan't be that unfair to Mrs. Robb. She testified that on the night of Mr. Bailey's arrival, 30 April, she had gone to bed at about half-past ten. Her husband had been called out to tend to a sick mare and she had therefore left the bedroom door unlatched. It was sometime shortly past midnight that she heard someone come into the room. She was greatly shocked when she heard the voice of the Rev. Bailey, and even more so when he begged that she permit him to "stay with her." She told him to leave immediately or she would tell her husband. He begged her not to, she recalled his exact words, "For God's sake, don't!" Mrs. Robb admitted that she did not tell her husband and, in fact, said nothing for another two weeks. She kept up this silence despite her claim that on two subsequent occasions he made lewd comments and tried to kiss her. It wasn't until 14 May that she did tell her husband. John Robb was enraged and confronted Mr. Bailey threatening to "chop his head off" if he didn't leave their house at once.

Robb followed his wife before the magistrates and supported her version of events. He said that once he had learned of Bailey's treachery, he ordered him out of the house. He told the curate that the rector would be informed directly. Robb said Bailey then offered him £20 for his silence, raising the offer eventually to £50.

The Rev. Mr. Bailey was present and his solicitor declared that the clergyman was fully ready to defend himself against these maliciously false charges. For the moment, however, he would be permitted only to make a plea of guilty or not guilty. The Rev. Bailey said firmly, "I am as innocent as any man in this court." Mr. Brook-Little begged the magistrates to dismiss the case on the grounds of simple implausibility. The tale told by Robb and his wife defied belief. A clergyman, in good standing, would hardly go roaming the halls of a strange and darkened house on his very first night in residence to attempt to seduce his landlady. But the magistrates felt that there was enough of a question that the case would have to be sent on to a grand jury at the upcoming quarter sessions. In the meantime, the accused would be permitted bail. The sureties were set at £50, a cost shared by the Rev. Mr. Ellis and a local farmer named George Brownlow.

The case against the Rev. Arthur Wellesley Bailey was called on 30 June 1898 at the Isle of Ely Quarter Sessions. The formal charge was that he "did unlawfully and indecently assault and ill-treat" Mrs. Mary Ann Robb.

The presiding magistrate was Thomas Fardell of Wisbech, a former MP, who declared the case a matter of "grave importance." To prosecute, Dr. John Cooper had come from Cambridge. Ernest Wild, a future judge, was then a young Norwich barrister and was to defend the accused clergyman. The courtroom, in a favourite phrase of the breathless press of the day, was again "crowded to suffocation."

As before, Mary Ann Robb opened the proceedings by recounting the events of the first night that the Rev. Bailey had slept under their roof. She provided some new details. Mary Ann said she had been shaken awake to find the man standing over her bed. The man's hand was under her blankets, shaking her thigh. She immediately ordered him to leave the room and vowed to tell her husband. He had begged her not to do so. She did not. The clergyman had then left Outwell for a few days for business in London but soon after his return he repeated his insulting conduct on at least two more occasions. On the 6th of May, he grabbed her by the waist and tried to kiss her. The last incident occurred on the 14th of the month. When she knocked at his door, having brought up his bath water, he called to her to enter and she found him naked. This insult was all she could bear. Her husband must be told. John became extremely angry and took her to confront the curate.

Though Mr. Bailey tried to deny it, her husband said he did not believe him and threatened to "chop his head off" if he didn't leave Outwell immediately. Mary Ann said she was sent to her mother's home until Mr. Bailey was gone.

Under questioning by Mr. Bailey's counsel, the farmer's wife said that the night of 30 April was very dark and the intruder came into the room without a candle. She believed that he was fully clothed. While she first thought it might have been her husband, when she heard the voice, she recognized it was their new lodger, the Rev. Bailey. She insisted that she had not told her husband at the very first opportunity because Mr. Bailey had apologized and vowed that there would be no repeat of his misconduct. She admitted that she did not tell her husband about the other incidents until two weeks had passed.

Mr. Wild: Why did you not tell your husband immediately? Why did you put up with this?
Mrs. Robb: I put up with it —-
Mr. Wild: Because you're an obliging landlady?
Mr. Cooper: Oh, no, we must have none of that!

Mrs. Robb conceded that she was ashamed that she not told her husband immediately but it was the truth.

Wild changed the subject to the state of the young couple's finances. Mrs. Robb admitted that they were in some straightened circumstances, hence the decision to take in a lodger. There had been one or two judgments taken out against them that remained unpaid. As she understood it, their lease on the farm was up at Michaelmas (the end of September) but she didn't think they stood any real chance of being evicted. Shortly after the Rev. Mr. Bailey took up his lodgings with the Robbs, he had to go to London for a funeral. Wild suggested that Mary Ann had been telling others in Outwell that her lodger had gone to bury his "very rich aunt." She said that she only knew that Mr. Bailey's aunt had died, and had not commented on any legacies that might be due him.

John Robb testified that his wife had not said a thing to him about Mr. Bailey's conduct until 14 May – a fortnight after the lodger's arrival. He had, however, noticed that Mary Ann was behaving strangely, very quiet and she seemed unusually low. On the 14th, he found her crying near the coal bin and she finally related the series of indecencies that she had suffered at the hands of the Rev. Mr. Bailey. He described himself as enraged. With his wife at his side, he confronted the clergyman and ordered him to get his bags and take his leave immediately. Robb said that Bailey pleaded with him, "What sort of tale am I to tell the people?" Robb said he replied that that was no concern of his. He then threatened to get a billhook and chop the curate's head off if he didn't get out of the house. [What must he, a clergyman who had lived amongst those who wielded the whirling blade of the chakra, have thought of this threat of beheading by a common farmer's billhook?] Robb said that Bailey had, in turn, accused Mary Ann of lying and said he would go to the police. The loyal husband said he was not afraid of that either; he believed his wife and, further, he would be writing a letter to the Rev. Ellis, the absent rector. He then took some of the clergyman's kit and threw it outside the door. Robb said that Bailey had then asked what he should do with the 35 shillings he owed the Robbs and John said he answered that he wouldn't keep him as a lodger for all the money in the Bank of England. Robb insisted that was the first and only time he had ever mentioned money in connection with this whole incident. That evening, according to Robb, a note arrived at the farm from Bailey offering to come by in the morning to settle up his outstanding bill. The curate wrote, "I want to pay your bill. I want to get the matter over with. I will treat you liberally." Cooper, the prosecutor, stressed that the only money Robb had ever demanded from the Rev. Bailey was the 35 shillings owed him for room and board. Cooper thought that was "very liberal, indeed." Mr. Wild quickly rose to complain that the prosecutor was playing to the gallery and it was really "quite a pity."

Mr. Bailey came to the cottage the following morning. Robb testified that he brought a letter for the farmer to sign. It was written in red ink and stated that Robb completely withdrew all the charges against him. The clergyman placed the letter in front of Robb and also placed on the table two £5 notes and £10 in gold coins. The money would be his, Robb said he was told, if he signed the statement. He refused. The clergyman said he would go as high as £50 but not a farthing more. Robb said he told Bailey that he would not take his money; he had written to the rector and was determined to wait upon Mr. Ellis' return. At which point, the Rev. Bailey took his leave and Robb said he had not heard from him again.

Robb having concluded this dramatic story of billhook threats and the violent ejection of his wife's assailant, was left to the clergyman's counsel. Wild asked him to explain why, before Mr. Bailey left the cottage, Robb had fixed him lunch? Robb admitted that he gave his departing lodger some ham, bread and cold water, before turning him out on the street. Mr. Wild asked for an explanation why a lunch was offered to the man who, only moments before, Robb had threatened to behead? Would a husband whose wife had been so insulted by a person have then prepared a meal for him?

Wild turned anew to the subject of the financial well being of farmer John Robb. There were outstanding judgments against him, the witness conceded. At present, he had been unable to pay them. The lease for the cottage he shared with his wife was up in ninety days. Robb insisted that the picture was not as dire as the clergyman's counsel was attempting to paint it. The crops were awaited. Something would surely turn up. Wild suggested that when the Robbs first approached their lodger with these false claims and demands for "hush money", it was Mr. Bailey who denied them immediately and left the cottage that very day. Robb denied the suggestion that he had been "laying a trap" for the hapless clergyman. Wild insisted that the Rev. Bailey had returned to Robb's cottage the following day simply to settle the bill and no more. If the curate had truly made these outlandish promises to pay £20 or even £50, wild sums to a poor Norfolk tenant farmer, enough to have settled all the Robb debts, why had Robb not just taken the money when offered? Robb stuck with his story. The farmer said he had decided to wait upon the returning rector. It made no sense.

The other witnesses for the prosecution were questioned only briefly. Charlotte Beeton, Mary Ann's mother, married now to the publican who kept the Bridge Inn, said she had urged her son-in-law not to sign any paper that Mr. Bailey had placed in front of him. Mrs. Beeton said the curate was defiant, boasting that they couldn't prove anything against him and besides, "You can only have me for the attempt."

For the defense, Mr. Wild's options were limited. Interestingly, as the Bailey case was being heard in Wisbech, the House of Commons was completing work on the Criminal Evidence Act of 1898. Soon, for the first time in Britain, the accused could – but not must – take the stand in his or her defense. In his trial, however, the Rev. Bailey's mouth was perforce sealed. The only witness called for the defense was the Rev. Henry Venn Ellis, rector of Outwell. He told the court that the Rev. Mr. Bailey had performed his clerical duties at St. Clement's quite well and there were no complaints against him from anyone in the village. Ellis had been staying in Bedford and testified to having received letters from both his curate and from John Robb. He read the latter's letter with alarm and concern. He was heartened by the letter he then received from the Rev. Bailey in which the curate blamed this unpleasantness on some "trifling money matters" which had arisen between himself and his former landlord. Any additional charges made by John Robb were a "total fabrication...without a vestige of truth." The curate said he would await the rector's return to make a full statement on the matter. Mr. Ellis said he had been happy to post a portion of the bail for his fellow cleric.

The testimony having taken all day, closing arguments were held over to a second day. The prosecutor, Dr. Cooper challenged the argument that such behaviour on Mr. Bailey's part was improbable. It may have been a strange house, but Mr. Bailey and Mary Ann were not strangers. He knew her from her church work. Perhaps, he fancied her. The deciding question, said Cooper, was why did Mr. Bailey offer to buy the Robb's silence? For the defense, Wild being unavailable; his co-counsel, James Brooke Little addressed the grand jurors. He admitted that Mr. Bailey had handled this matter poorly, even calling his client "a fool in many matters." But a clergyman cannot "brave it out" as might an ordinary man; there must not even be a breath of scandal. Even false accusations will be damaging. On the other hand, the Robb's story, argued Brooke-Little, rang false from the very first night. In a strange house, in the dark, without a candle, a hitherto innocent clergyman becomes a roaming lothario? Even Mr. Robb had testified that when he came to bed that night, his wife was sound asleep. Brooke-Little asked the jurymen, "After such an outrage … is it possible for a modest woman (and I am not suggesting that she is not a modest woman) to be sweetly sleeping when her husband comes to bed two hours later?"

Addressing his grand jury, magistrate Fardell, summed up the case with a decided tilt towards the side of the accused clergyman. He said allegations such as the Robbs had placed before them were quite easy to make and extremely difficult to disprove. For any man, more especially for a clergyman, to be convicted of such a crime would be ruinous to career and reputation. The jury would need to consider the accusers very carefully. Was John Robb a man to be believed? The defense had accused him of extortion. Robb was certainly a man in need of money thereby giving him a motive for such a crime. To believe his story would require supportive evidence. As for Mary Ann Robb, her silence for two weeks in the face of repeated assaults was inexplicable. Why had she not cried out that first night?

Of course, Fardell might have pointed out that there was no one home that night but an infant son. How far away was the ailing mare that John Robb had gone to attend?

The grand jury, taking the instructions to heart, took very little time at their work. Jackson, the jury foreman, reported back that, owing to the contradictory evidence, they were unable to return a true bill against the Rev. A.W. Bailey. According to *The Wisbech Standard*, "almost everybody in the court commenced a very animated conversation with his neighbour." It took a stern demand for order to silence the murmurs. Regardless, the Rev. Mr. Bailey was free to leave the Wisbech court. He would also have to leave Outwell. He had been cleared only for lack of evidence and his usefulness for any clerical duties in the area was gone.

Bailey would find new assignments: at first, in the village of Ripple in Kent, then to Birmingham, and so on. Again, he stayed a year or two at each place. In 1909, he was a curate at St. Martin's in London where he remained until 1916, his longest stay at any church in his career. He disappears from Crockford's Clerical Directory in 1933.

John and Mary Ann Robb, their story disbelieved, also left Outwell. Perhaps, that lease was not renewed at Michaelmas. In the 1901 census, the Robbs had moved to Walsoken, a village directly outside Wisbech, some few miles from their old farmhouse.

In time, the curate's lawyer became Sir Ernest Wild and sat on the criminal bench where he was a scourge to blackmailers of any stripe. In March of 1927, he sentenced a 25-year old motor driver to seven years in prison for blackmailing a clergyman, having bled the un-named cleric of £1400. Sir Ernest declared, "There is no more deadly injury that one human being can do to another than blackmail – it was the murder of the soul, the assassination of the mind."

Some Little Latitude

The Rev. Thomas Berney,
Rector of Bracon Ash

SIMON JENKINS, in his wonderful book, *England's Thousand Best Churches*, is a great admirer of Norfolk. "There are churches everywhere, beckoning the eye with great windows, high clerestories and rich carvings, and beckoning the ear with bells." All of that, of course, is true. We shall, however, concern ourselves with two of the smaller and more obscure churches in the county that can only beckon the reader with a great story.

Not a million miles southwest of Norwich (more like six miles) you will find the quaintly named Norfolk village of Bracon Ash. The church of St. Nicholas is small, it has no tower, and worshippers are summoned by the ringing of a single bell. If anything is remarkable about the church in Bracon Ash at all, it is the attached Berney Mausoleum. One of the oldest and proudest of Norfolk landowning families – Berneys had been lords of the manor here since the mid 18th century. In 1860, the lord of the manor was the Rev. Thomas Berney, who was also rector of the church of St. Nicholas. He lived in Bracon Hall, built in 1833 to replace the old manor house that had once played host to Elizabeth I. A brick mansion, the new Bracon Hall was later to be grudgingly acknowledged by Mr. Pevsner to be "nice." As for the rector, Mr. Berney, with no more than 280

souls under his care, his burdens were not so tiring that he could not
devote a good deal of his time to his divers other interests. Mr. Berney
was amassing one of Europe's great collections of Italian majolica, he had
a well-stocked library, he loved to garden, he loved to paint and, upon
occasion, he spoke directly to the Lord. It was Mr. Berney's pleasure to
inform all that "the Lord Jesus Christ had appeared unto me on January
8th, 1854." The eccentric Mr. Berney was unmarried, in his early 40's, and
resided at the Hall with his widowed mother.

To the north of Bracon Ash, across a field or two, perhaps a mile and a
quarter away you will find what was then, and is today, the "scattered"
village of East Carleton. It is difficult to see how the village could ever
have supported two churches. To be sure, the old St. Peter's church had
fallen down, leaving now only the small flint and rubble church of St.
Mary, with a modest tower. The church you will see today is almost
entirely the result of a late Victorian restoration directed by the rector, the
Rev. James John Cumming. Mr. Cumming first arrived in East Carleton in
1860. His late father had been a famously eccentric Cambridge don. Mr.
Cumming was 35 and newly married; his wife Helen was the daughter of
a prominent businessman (and a future mayor) of King's Lynn. East
Carleton must have been one of the stranger places in the Church of
England, for while it had two churches, St. Mary – where Mr. Cumming
would now officiate - and St. Peter (albeit in ruins), it had no livable
accommodations for the rector and his wife. However, back across those
fields, adjacent to St. Nicholas church in Bracon Ash, the rectory there
stood unoccupied. Mr. Berney, as we know, was comfortably housed at the
Hall, and he graciously arranged to rent his rectory to Mr. and Mrs.
Cumming.

The Cummings were quite happy at Bracon rectory. In 1862, their first
child, a son named James Stuart, was born. Bracon was quite convenient
to St. Mary's; by foot or on horseback, it was but a short journey to Mr.
Cumming's church. The footpaths across the field would bring Mr.
Cumming directly past the Hall and there was much convivial society
between the two churchmen. It also soon became clear that Mr. Berney
and Mrs. Cumming shared a similar interest. They were both avid
gardeners; while Mr. Berney had his greenhouse, Mrs. Cumming was
keenly devoted to her flowerbeds. Mr. Berney would often come to the
rectory to paint the flora in their more natural setting. Three years pleasantly passed for all with many teas to be drunk and sandwiches to be
nibbled under the shade of the trees in the park at the Hall.

When the happy idyll had ended, Mr. Cumming would recall that he had sometimes felt that Mr. Berney was, in truth, too often at the rectory. It might have seemed even that Mr. Berney, with his brushes & easel, contrived to stay till the last light of a Norfolk evening and – then, out of courtesy and much to their credit – the Cummings would ask him to stay for supper before his short walk back to the Hall. Of course, these were the thoughts of Mr. Cumming after the events of the spring of 1864.

That April, Mrs. Cumming's sister came to stay at Bracon Ash. Maria Elizabeth Durrant was 18 and was happy to be called "Bessie" by all who knew her. The young lady's arrival would bring a dramatic end to these pretty "scenes of clerical life." The storm broke soon after an incident at a picnic on 14 June. That evening, Bessie told her sister that she didn't want to be left alone any longer with Mr. Berney. Earlier that day, he had cornered her on a sofa and she had to tell him that if he didn't move away from her, she would have to scream. Bessie also disclosed to her sister that two weeks before, while she was over at the Hall, Mr. Berney had kissed her in the library. Mrs. Cumming went to her husband, to relay Bessie's accusations and – also, for the first time – to confess to him that on at least two occasions, she too had been the victim of Mr. Berney's unwanted importunings, to the point of his twice asking her to make love with him.

Could this be true? Mr. Cumming, a good husband believing in his good wife, wrote immediately to Mr. Berney. Since the recipient never revealed the contents of the letter, nor could Mr. Cumming produce a copy, the exact contents of the letter can only be imagined. However, here is Mr. Berney's reply:

> I was so much irritated on receiving your letter that I dared not trust myself to write. It is generally admitted that where two persons are much thrown together and daily meeting in mirth and fun, some little latitude is allowable, though the extent be perhaps as various as the sets of which society is composed. Nothing can be farther from my wish than to give offence by exceeding its proper limits; and I am anxious to offer a most sincere apology for anything in which I may have offended. The society of your relatives has ever been a source of real happiness to me, and nothing can exceed my sorrow that anything should have occurred to mar the harmony which existed; and my heartfelt wish is, that the apology thus sincerely offered, may be accepted.

Mr. Cumming objected to the tone of Mr. Berney's reply, perhaps he stood not totally in agreement with the suggestion that "some little latitude" with another man's wife might occasionally be permissible. Mr. Cumming decided that he was duty bound to refer the matter to the Bishop of Norwich. The result was that the Rev. Thomas Berney, rector of Bracon Ash, was to be formally charged with using lewd and incontinent language and "soliciting the chastity" of Mrs. John Cumming and her sister Maria Elizabeth Durrant.

By the time Dr. Stephen Lushington, dean of the Court of Arches, convened the proceedings to hear the charges against Rev. Berney another two years had passed. Twas ever true the legal process moves slowly and the ecclesiastical courts – with their rules and ritual – even more so. There were, of course, efforts to settle this unpleasant matter without a public trial that could only be an embarrassment to the participants and a scandal to the church. Mr. Berney was barely co-operative; he maintained his innocence from the first and challenged the need for such a trial, based on the unsupported words of his two female accusers. He also asserted that the procedure was inherently unfair, as he well knew that in the Arches Court, he would not be allowed to testify in his own behalf. Mr. Cumming and the women from the rectory had also been unmoved by any requests that they recant or mitigate their stories.

In May 1866, the Rev. James John Cumming was the first witness to be called in the trial of *Bishop of Norwich v. Berney*. He testified to the reason why he was in residence at the rectory in Bracon Ash, the friendship established with Rev. Berney which was enjoyed by himself, his wife and her sister, and the shocking intelligence of Mr. Berney's misconduct that he received from his wife for the first time in June of 1864.

Helen Mary Cumming was called. Dr. James Parker Deane was counsel for the prosecutors, representing the church and – in effect – Mrs. Cumming and Miss Durrant. Deane led Mrs. Cumming through a recounting of the "happy times" in Bracon Ash and her relationship with Mr. Berney, the gardens, the flowers, the teas, etc. She said this all changed on 10 May 1864 when, after luncheon, she found herself alone at Bracon rectory with Mr. Berney. Mr. Cumming and Miss Durrant were out riding. Mrs. Cumming was a woman with many health complaints for whom riding was too strenuous. She testified that Mr. Berney – without warning - said to her, "Come on the sofa with me; the blinds are drawn. Mr. Cumming will never know anything about it." Mrs. Cumming recalled that she was literally staggered by this sudden entreaty and very nearly fainted. Mr. Berney had to get her a chair. Recovering herself, Mrs. Cumming told the clergyman, "How can you talk to me in such a way? Do you not know that I am a married woman – and yet you, a clergyman, wish me to commit such a sin?" Mr. Berney continued to press the matter. He said, "If you let me have my way with you, as I hope for salvation, I will never say a word of it." At that point, she implored him to leave and warned, "If you ever do this again, I shall tell my husband." To which, she testified, Mr. Berney coolly responded, "Oh, no, you won't." And, in fact, she didn't.

The second incident involving Mrs. Cumming and the rector of Bracon Ash took place eleven days later. It was 21 May, a Saturday. She again found herself alone with Mr. Berney, this time in the rectory dining room. She stated that the clergyman again used his opportunity to behave and express himself very improperly.

He indicated that he had something to say and didn't want the servants coming in and out, but she told him that she was not afraid of her servants knowing anything she did or said. He then jumped to his feet and closed the door to the kitchen. She recalled his exact words, "I want something so very bad; I've been so excited all the week; do let me have my own way." Again, she pleaded that he must desist from such flagrant misconduct. Her voice became so loud that Mr. Berney warned her that the servants might overhear. She ordered him to leave her at once, telling him "If you continue to behave like this, either you or I shall have to leave Bracon Ash." Mr. Berney agreed to take his leave but not before making a final shocking comment, "You know, a slice out of a cut cake will never be missed." Mrs. Cumming testified that then the Rev. Berney apprised her, "I shall go home and make a fool of myself with Susan (his housekeeper) or someone else." Though aghast at Mr. Berney's language and behaviour, Helen Cumming still did not think it proper that she inform her husband.

The next day was Trinity Sunday. Mrs. Cumming testified that she and her sister both took Holy Communion on that feast day. However, she insisted that the sacrament was not administered on that occasion by the Rev. Thomas Berney.

Mrs. Cumming was next to be questioned by Dr. Travers Twiss, representing Mr. Berney. He asked her to identify a letter, received by Mr. Berney on the 16th of May, less than a week following the first "let me have my way with you" encounter. Yes, she had written that letter. The letter had to do with some issues about the use of a harmonium and thanking Mr. Berney for the gift of a vase. Dr. Twiss then read some of Mrs. Cumming's words aloud:

> You could scarcely have had more lovely weather for gardening … I shall be anxious to hear how you get on … Mr. Cumming & Bessie unite with me in very kind regards and believe me, yours sincerely, Helen M. Cumming

Was this the letter from a woman to a gentleman who had – as she had testified – so grossly insulted her not a week previous? She was also asked to be especially certain as to from whom she took communion on Trinity Sunday. Mrs. Cumming continued to insist that she did not receive the sacrament from the hands of Mr. Berney.

The next witness was Maria Elizabeth Durrant. She had come to stay at the rectory at Bracon Ash in April. She had been much in the society of Rev. Berney and had had no reason to object to his conduct until 29 May. It was a Sunday and after the day's services, Bessie recalled being out walking with her sister, when Mr. Berney invited them to see his greenhouse. Mrs. Cumming, feeling poorly, declined the invitation but Bessie agreed to join Mr. Berney in viewing the spring flowers. After some little time in the greenhouse, Mr. Berney asked if she would like to come into the library to see some of his new designs. There, amidst one of the finest private collections in Norfolk, the Rev. Berney suddenly put his arms around her waist and kissed her. Pulling herself free, Bessie testified that she scolded Mr. Berney and said she would have to go home at once. She said Mr. Berney urged her to stay, "You need not be afraid, I won't hurt you or get you in any trouble." He suggested that they go upstairs into the drawing room. She refused. He persisted, "Oh, nonsense. Do come." Instead, Bessie testified that she opened the door and left Bracon Hall with Mr. Berney following her part of the way towards the rectory. Upset greatly by what had occurred, Bessie decided that, nonetheless, she could not reveal to anyone what had happened while she was alone in the company of her sister's great friend up in the Hall.

Finally, we come to the events of 14 June. There had been a picnic attended by all and, in the evening, Mr. Berney was in the drawing room of the rectory, where (what good fortune!) he found himself again alone with Miss Durrant. Bessie testified that she declined his invitation to sit with him on the sofa. He then stood up and took her by the arm, kissed her and attempted to pull her down on to the sofa beside him. Bessie recalled telling him, "Let me go or I'll scream." Again, the wretched cleric had been frustrated. No doubt the chance having been missed, the evening ended uncomfortably. Mr. Berney soon disconsolately trudged back to the Hall. That night, Bessie told her sister privately that she no longer wanted to be left alone in Mr. Berney's company and she told of both the incident in the Hall library and in their own drawing room. Helen decided that, at last, Mr. Cumming would have to be told.

The testimony of the two women and their recollections of the series of incidents made up the case in full against the Rev. Thomas Berney. For the defense, Dr. Twiss called the parish clerk who testified that Mr. Berney had, in fact, distributed Holy Communion on the feast day. Several servants – at both the rectory and the Hall - were called to say they saw or heard nothing during any of these emotional and libidinous confrontations. He also produced the usual witnesses of stature to testify to their confidence that the Mr. Berney they knew would never have conducted himself in such a manner.

In his closing statement, Dr. Twiss took three hours to present his defense for Rev. Berney, raising several issues. He said the two-year time lapse in bringing the charges had been extremely unfair to his client in preparation for this trial. The charges themselves were vague. Most importantly, however, Mr. Berney, he insisted, stood ready to deny everything under oath, but under the rules of the Arches, he could not testify. Twiss reminded Dr. Lushington that only a few years before, the Dean had similarly refused to hear the testimony of a Dorset curate accused of raping a schoolmistress. In that case, however, Lushington had freed the curate because the woman's story was uncorroborated. The testimony of both Mrs. Cumming and Miss Durrant was here again completely uncorroborated. No servants at either the Hall or the rectory saw anything or heard anything. As for the letter that Mr. Berney sent to Mr. Cumming, Twiss argued that in no way should it be read as corroboration or an apology; instead, it was the first reaction of a man completely caught off guard by these wild accusations.

Mrs. Cumming, Twiss asserted, was the key to the entire case. Why did she not tell her husband about Mr. Berney's behaviour immediately? Instead, she writes a letter to Mr. Berney in which she's "anxious" to hear from him and sends "kind regards." Then, after the second try, why would she take communion from the hands of a man who the very day before had used an expression so coarse as, "A slice out of a cut cake is never missed?" Finally, and quite inexplicably, why would she – on the

29th of May – walk away and leave her innocent 18-year old sister in this man's company, knowing what she did?

For the prosecutors, Dr Deane argued that if there had been undue delays, they were the fault of Mr. Berney's own obstruction. The defendant had hoped to the last to forestall the shocking testimony that had just been given. Could anyone possibly believe that these two respectable women would "without any assignable motive" hatch such a "vile scheme" against a respected clergyman to whom they owed, however temporarily, the roof over their heads? Would they then commit gross perjury? Mrs. Cumming, from the best of motives, not wishing to cause a quarrel, had determined not to reveal to her husband the details of Mr. Berney's conduct. As a married woman, she felt equipped to deal with these insults but, when her young sister, a guest in their home, was subjected to similar advances, Mrs. Cumming acted with dispatch. Deane also suggested that Mr. Berney and his family might have tampered with witnesses, including the parish clerk. As to the Trinity Sunday services, it made no difference to the case whether Mr. Berney administered the sacrament or not. There was no evidence that Helen and Bessie knew in advance which clergyman would have that responsibility and, if it was Mr. Berney, to have left the church or refused to approach would have caused much comment. As for the servants, many were called but why not Susan Basey, Mr. Berney's housekeeper? Had he gone home that day and "made a fool of himself" with her? Had he ever done so before? As for Mr. Berney's letter in response to Mr. Cumming, did he not use the word "apology?" Was that the letter of an innocent man? Why did he not indignantly deny the charges? Instead, he tried to flippantly excuse his wanton behaviour as a "little latitude."

Dr. Lushington took several days to consider his verdict. He decided that the evidence of the incidents did not require corroboration. Presumably, he was willing to put more faith in the testimony of a clergyman's wife and her sister than in the accusations of a Dorset schoolmistress. The Dean also said he had observed the women "very carefully" during their testimony, looking for any indication that they were intending to "exaggerate, conceal or tamper" with their statements and he found there none. He concluded that Mrs. Cumming and the winsome Miss Durrant were upright and believable witnesses. He did not think Mrs. Cumming had acted wisely in deciding not to inform her husband immediately upon the first alleged approach by Mr. Berney. Of course, he conceded, she is certainly not the first lady to remain silent in such an affair. The question for Lushington was then "whether such concealment tends to shew she was guilty of false swearing. I cannot think it does." He also found Mr. Berney's epistolary response to the charges inappropriate and not a letter that was written by a man confident of his innocence. In the end, the Dean ruled that the charges had been substantially proven. Though it pained him, he ordered that the Rev. Thomas Berney be suspended *ab officio et beneficio* for a period of two years. Dr. Twiss immediately announced that the case would be appealed.

In the interval, the press reaction to the suspension was generally unfavourable. For instance, *The Examiner* suggested:

> [Rev. Berney's] bold animal overtures might be ascribed to innocence in intrigue, but there was in it a degree of shamelessness which suggested a hardened sinner. What is there to turn the wolf into a safe shepherd, who can be trusted with men's wives and sisters without fear of the contamination of libidinous solicitations and advances?

Another seven months would pass before the appeal of *Berney v. Bishop of Norwich* was called in February 1867. Appeals from the Court of Arches were heard by the Lords of the Privy Council. Mr. Berney's case was assigned to Sir William Erle, a veteran jurist and, interestingly, the son of a Dorset clergyman himself. Erle, who had recently retired, was known for his unquestioned impartiality as much as his "urbanity." To be sure, however, what might be excused as urbanity in London might not be tolerated in the drawing room of a Norfolk country rectory. In a case before the Privy Council, there would be no need for the rectory ladies to subject themselves again to rehearsing those frightful moments in Mr. Berney's company; the full record of the Arches Court testimony was in front of Mr. Justice Erle.

The appeal was solely on the issue of corroboration. Dr. Twiss, once again representing Mr. Berney, now "the appellant," argued that the Dean had been wrong to accept the uncorroborated testimony of Mrs. Cumming and Miss Durrant. Dr. Deane, once again for the Bishop and the rectory people, pointed out that, unlike Justice Erle, Dr. Lushington had had the advantage of observing the women carefully as they gave their evidence and he accepted their testimony as believable. Mr. Berney's letter of "apology" was also confirmation of his lewd and incontinent conduct with these two innocent women.

Justice Erle took over three weeks to consider the case and then summoned the parties back for his ruling. He opened by criticizing the Dean of Arches for his decision to rely solely on the word of Mrs. Cumming and Miss Durrant. As he put it, a "tribunal ill-performs its duty if it adopts as true every statement on oath not contradicted on counter-testimony." Having put that matter to rest, Erle decided that he would now review the testimony of the two women for himself. Were their accounts probably true? Did Mrs. Cumming actually believe that the Rev. Berney was proposing – on either occasion - that she and he immediately commit adultery? He found that idea to be completely improbable. Such behaviour would "shock any but a known profligate, that is, immediate adultery in mid-day, in a room comparatively open to interruption." Further, Mrs. Cumming's recollection of the exact words used by Mr. Berney, repeated by her word for word on more than one occasion, struck the old veteran of the criminal bench as suspect. In his experience, it was "very rare" for a witness to recall another person's exact words, let alone their own. And what of Mrs. Cumming's letter to Mr. Berney, written six days after he begged her to "let me have my way with you?" It was not the letter of an aggrieved woman but rather one that displayed "unalloyed favourable feelings and a desire for the continuation of friendly intercourse and correspondence." Justice Erle said he could only presume from that letter that Mrs. Cumming had no reason to be angry with Rev. Berney until *after* her sister had complained of his conduct. While stopping short of accusing her of perjury, he ruled that the charges brought by Mrs. Cumming against Mr. Berney had not been sufficiently proved.

Turning next to Miss Durrant's allegations, Justice Erle said it was important to remember that both the young woman and Mr. Berney were single adults. In the spring of 1864, she was 18 and he was 46, by no means an age difference that would trouble an urbane Victorian judge:

> The parties were on such terms that the appellant might properly make advances to the lady if she chose to accept them and if in doing so he transgressed the bounds of good manners and decorum and so gave offence, it does not follow that he had the guilt which the offended parties going back over that which had passed without notice at the time, chose to impute.

Somewhere in there, amidst the convoluted language of the day, can be found the legal theory that "There's no harm in asking." From where

Justice Erle sat, Mr. Berney's conduct toward Miss Bessie was "capable of a less guilty construction."

The testimony of wife and sister having been set aside, Mr. Justice Erle concluded by discharging the Rev. Thomas Berney from the previous edict of suspension and clearing him to resume his duties at the church of St. Nicholas, Bracon Ash.

Let's try to imagine what might have really happened in this small corner of Norfolk in the spring of 1864. The arrival of Miss Bessie Durrant seems to have been the cause of it all. Young and, for argument's sake, we'll say attractive, and from a good family, it is safe to say that eligible females like Bessie were not likely thick on the ground in greater Bracon Ash. It is quite likely that the middle-aged clergyman became hopelessly besotted with the maiden visitor. She would be the *chatelaine* that Bracon Hall truly needed. He guided her through his greenhouse, delighted in explaining his priceless majolica, and then, there in his library, amid the light of a spring afternoon, his emotions betrayed him. A sudden embrace and a kiss, a few murmured youthful "No's" and, as quickly, she was gone. Reproaching himself, no doubt, for his premature sally, Mr. Berney surely told himself that all was not lost and a new opportunity would present itself, to quote him, "where two persons are much thrown together and daily meeting in mirth and fun." After the picnic on 14 June, a day that presumably featured more mirth and more fun, a heartened Mr. Berney tried again and was rebuffed a second time. Plainly the "pull her down on the sofa" approach was not one that Bessie found compelling. She would have to seek advice from her big sister on how to deal with this man.

Helen Cumming is the enigma in all of this. While Mr. Berney's unrequited passion for the youthful Bessie can be excused and is the stuff of drawing room comedy, his ham-handed bid, not once, but twice, to seduce a brother clergyman's wife is much more melodramatic. Can Mrs. Cumming be telling the truth? Firstly, what possible motive would she have for lying about it? To have simply told her husband that Mr. Berney's attentions to Bessie were not welcome was one thing. Mr. Cumming could have dealt with that discreetly, perhaps not without some bruised feelings on the rejected swain's part, but handled as between two gentlemen. Why invent the additional charges that he "solicited her chastity," which she likely knew would raise the matter from an awkward parish muddle to the level of a "scandal to the church?" As the counsel for the Bishop said in the first trial, why would such a respectable woman concoct such a "vile scheme?" Jealousy is a possibility; had she and Mr.

Berney established some private intimacy, however tame it likely was? Did she feel betrayed when he so quickly transferred his ardor to her younger sister? Was it resentment? From a prominent family, married to the son of a Cambridge don, here she was stuck in a dismal "scattered village" in rural Norfolk, she and her husband living as tenants, while Mr. Berney, literally, lorded it over them from his fancy Hall. Perhaps she was mentally unbalanced; we don't know. Mr. Berney's counsel would certainly have put the matter of her mental state into play if that were indeed the case. Perhaps the picture of the pre-Bessie idyll in Bracon Ash was a myth. Might Mr. Berney have been a nuisance to the Cummings and their toddler son, dropping in all the time and staying to dinner? Might he have put on his condescending "Berney airs"? Conceivably, he might have made a private remark or two in Mrs. Cumming's company that he might have considered acceptable with "some little latitude" but she found "lewd and incontinent." However, I cannot believe that Mr. Berney, absent any other evidence of a propensity for such conduct, and with Bessie now in residence, another person to overhear or walk in, would – after four blameless years – blurt out his desire to roger his neighbour's wife.

That said, what of Mr. Berney's mental state? Was he more than a little bit "off" and capable of random acts of offensive behaviour? There was no evidence from any other women who had any complaints about his behaviour. Is there any more reason to suspect that a man who was capable of believing and acting upon "visions" and "prophecies" would misconduct himself in his personal life? Soon after he had been cleared of the charges against him, Berney published a book of prophecies being a collection of bizarre visions "vouchsafed unto him." Apparently, Mr. Berney spent a good deal of his time at the Carlton Club in London where he, no doubt, bored the members with the details of his "visions." On one occasion, a member of the club told him that he was considering a run for a seat in the House of Commons but did not know he might fare. Mr. Berney "at length prayed that a vision might be vouchsafed unto me." That night, he beheld bunches of grapes, to the right and the left. He knew (somehow) that the smaller bunch to the right represented those who would vote for his friend.

> I therefore told my friend the Vision; and that I knew from it, that, if he contested the Borough, he would have no chance of success. And he was satisfied.

Thus are great political careers made or lost.

Far beyond such trivialities, however, the greater purpose for Berney's book of Prophecies was to warn against attacks on the established church. Whether it be disestablishment in Ireland or the relaxation of the religious "tests" to attend Oxford and Cambridge, he believed he had been chosen by God who "set me as a watchman unto this country." He dedicated the book to Prime Minister Gladstone, who, if he ever read it, would have learned of Mr. Berney's vision of an England overrun by "Frogs, toads and water newts." Translating for the P.M., Mr. Berney explained that the toads are symbols of Papists and the water newts represent all sorts of immoralities. And the frogs? The French, of course.

Barmy, yes; lecherous, not proven, Mr. Berney remained at his little church and in residence at the Hall, until his sudden death in 1895 at the age of 77. His body lies now in the church in the attached Berney mausoleum, dismissed by Mr. Pevsner as "quite a stately, if ponderous, affair." And leaking now, as well, having been shown around the old church in 2007 by Rev. Jess Stubbleford, the team rector now based in Mulbarton.

An interesting note before closing: Maria Durrant, "dear Bessie," despite her apparent narrow escape from the clutches of the lecherous Mr. Berney, was not put off clergymen for good. In fact, she married one. In 1870 she and the Rev. George Croke Robinson were wed.

As for Mr. Cumming, he and his wife had, of course, already decamped from Bracon rectory – which was soon let to the rector of Fundenhall. (Safely let, as well, for Mr. Sedger was a widower with four children!) However, Mr. Cumming did not leave East Carleton. He remained rector there, only one uneasy mile across the fields from Bracon Hall, for another four decades. By then, the Cummings had taken lodgings in Heigham, Norwich, a few miles more distant but still quite close to St. Mary's. Their second child, a daughter, Margaret Helen was born in 1868. The parishioners - assisted by money from a Norwich charity – finally built a rectory for Mr. Cumming and St. Mary's in 1881. It is unlikely that Mr. Berney was ever invited for tea.

None of Us Trusts the Rev. Mr. Black

The Rev. Alured E. Black, Rector of Buxton

A bequest to a clergyman made by someone subject to his personal influence was always going to give rise to comment in Victorian England. Of course, clergymen were not alone under this focus of suspicion.

> A gift to a clergyman, confessor, physician, surgeon, solicitor, agent, butler [Bring me a pen and paper, Bunter!] or, in fact, to any person whose situation gives him an opportunity of acquiring an undue influence, may be impeached.

However, the unique role of a clergyman or similar spiritual adviser, standing nearby at a time when the dying person must confront "the other side," raised the concern to a higher standing. The probate courts were, of necessity then, to be vigilant "to prevent the undue influence which was likely to be exercised at the time of death for pious uses."

There was the famous case of the Rev. Mr. Prince of the infamous Agapemone (or, as the cynics dubbed it "I Gape for Money) movement.

The will of one of the dotty trio of Nottidge sisters enriching the sect was successfully challenged. In another case in London, a dissenting clergyman convinced a wealthy old woman, apparently quite insane, that by way of thanks for her great bequest, the Son of God would appear in her drawing room in Hyde Park Terrace. The will was thrown out. So taxing had it become for a clergyman to benefit under a will that some testators opted to leave their favourite clergymen out or pass on merely token bequests. In 1900, one rather brazen cleric in Nottinghamshire advised the woman who had planned to leave him £100 that it was hardly worth it. People would only say that he must not have been much of a friend. She must either leave him more or nothing at all lest they become a laughing stock. The woman then wrote a new will with a much larger bequest for her reverend companion; it was promptly tossed under the rule of "undue influence."

It is not breaking new ground to reveal that the chancery and probate courts of Victorian England were crowded with lawsuits over a dearly beloved's last will and testament. The Thelussons, Bagots, Tichbornes and families of their ilk, spent thousands of pounds to propound or to challenge wills establishing rights to great fortunes. But they were hardly alone; those with only the most modest of expectations also crowded the courts. Generations of sons and daughters, wives [and more than a few mistresses] as well as other assorted claimants have shuffled into court seeking redress and, to be sure, a nice bequest. On uncomfortable benches they were made to sit quietly and listen to bewigged barristers argue in a language known only to the practitioners of this quite lucrative, but very dreary, niche of the law. So dreary in fact, that Thomas Jarman of New Court, London, while compiling his magisterial *Treatise on Wills*, admitted that his "health more than once sank."

Sadly, when Mr. Jarman's health sank for the last time, in 1860, it was discovered to the great embarrassment of his profession – he had died without a will.

Miss Anne Cleland, a wealthy Irish spinster, was not one to leave this world without her wishes being made satisfactorily clear. Miss Cleland had a good-sized fortune of some £8000 (multiply by forty for a rough modern equivalent). At her death in 1894, her will was probated and it was her stated wish that her entire estate should pass to her niece, Annie Black. This most fortunate beneficiary was 34; Annie was the wife of the Rev. Alured Elliot Black, the vicar of Buxton, a small village on the river Bure, just northwest of Norwich.

Clergymen, as we have already stated, must be prepared to answer suspicions about a will made to their benefit. Thus it was in November 1895. The always sensational claim was made that the Rev. Mr. Black had used his clerical wiles to pressure a poor dying woman to tear up her previous will and, instead, he had cajoled the old spinster to leave her entire fortune to his wife. It was a case fit for a West End melodrama with the audience quite ready to hiss the skulking villain in his canonical black.

In 1895, the Rev. Alured (a form of the fine old English name of Alfred that sadly now more resembles a typo) Black was 36. He had been born in Norwich, the son of Col. George Black, who, for almost thirty years, was the Chief Constable of the county. His mother was the daughter of Admiral Sir John Marshall of Kent. Alured had been educated at Westminster and Trinity College, Cambridge. His clerical career began after his ordination in 1883. He spent several years in Thameside communites: four years at Holy Trinity Church, Blackheath Hill in Greenwich and then three as rector of the church of Sts. Peter & Paul in the village of Milton-next-Gravesend. In 1889, he came to Buxton, along with his wife Annie and their three children.

Prior to his ordination, Alured had worked as a tutor at a small school in Hereford. There he met a young Irishman by the name of John Warnock Cleland. In 1883, he became engaged to the lad's sister, 22-year old Annie Cleland. Alured was 23. The Clelands were a family of considerable property from County Down in Northern Ireland. The family owned more than 3500 acres near the community of Tobar Mhuire. The holdings were sizeable enough for the Clelands to be numbered among the families listed in Bateman's 1880 edition of *The Acre-ocracy of Great Britain & Ireland*. During the discussions leading up to Alured's wedding, the groom's father, a good old Norfolk "plod," admitted that his son did not have the fortune to match his bride's. Not to worry, he was assured, for Annie was the favoured niece of Aunt Anne Cleland. 65 years old, unmarried, and with a fortune of her own, Miss Anne had written to Col. Black assuring him that she intended to "leave her niece independent." It was indeed a fine catch for the young clergyman to make. Alured and Annie were married in Ireland on 14 November 1883.

The couple's first child, a daughter, Louise, was born in 1885, in Greenwich, where the Rev. Mr. Black was then serving as a curate. Aunt Anne came to stay with the young couple for the happy occasion. While she was in England, Miss Cleland took steps to fulfill her earlier promise; she consulted a solicitor who prepared a will leaving her entire fortune, "absolutely," to her niece, Mrs. Annie Black. There matters would stand until 1888.

Miss Cleland, as wealthy aunts can sometimes be, was somewhat mercurial. After her stay with the Blacks, she went home to Ireland. Whilst back in County Down, for reasons never quite made clear, she decided to have a new will drawn up by her brother-in-law, John Warnock, a prominent solicitor in Downpatrick. She was now of the mind that her fortune should be divided equally, with half going to Mrs. Black and the other half to Annie's younger sister, Florence Gertrude Cleland. This would have reduced the inheritance for the clergyman's wife by, at least, the sizeable figure of some £4000. Aunt Anne had not finished tinkering. In the following year, while still residing in County Down, Miss Anne attached a codicil stating her intention to forgive her nephew James, (the younger brother of Annie & Gertrude) a debt of nearly £2000. This act of generosity would further reduce the value of that portion of the Cleland fortune that would eventually come to the wife of the Rev. Mr. Black.

By now, Mr. Black had come to his new church in Buxton. His predecessor, the Rev. William Stracey-Clitheroe had been the rector in the village, with the adjoining parish of Oxnead, for nearly forty years. Of a prominent county family, the old rector had restored the 13th century church of St. Andrew. In addition, Rev. Mr. Stracey-Clitheroe had built a grand new rectory, complete with a squash court and, a rarity to be sure, a swimming pool. It was a roomy establishment: the 1891 census shows that the Rev. Alured Black and his wife Annie, were in residence with their two daughters, Louisa and Geraldine, and their 3 year old son, George, named for the now deceased former county constable. The Rev. Black's widowed mother was also living at the rectory. There was even enough room in the rectory ménage for the Blacks to accommodate their favourite aunt, 73-year old Anne Cleland, of County Down.

Miss Anne had come to stay in Buxton; she would remain there until her death from cancer in April of 1894. Following her death, a new will was presented to the probate court – signed by Miss Anne – and properly attested, in which the testatrix had revoked the earlier 50-50 will of 1888, and the ensuing codicil. Miss Anne Cleland had apparently, at the end, opted to revert to her earlier stated intention to leave her entire property to Mrs. Alured Black.

When the will was opened, the disappointment felt in the hearts and expectations of James Cleland and his sister Florence (now married to a

James Stirling) can easily be appreciated. Their aunt had chosen to cut them out of a will valued at some £8000, and would instead leave it all to their sister. James, with Florence's complete acquiescence, now produced a copy of the earlier will and codicil and insisted that it represented the true wishes of the late Miss Anne Cleland. It was his claim that the will that had now been produced by Mr. and Mrs. Black, at the eleventh hour, had been coaxed from a dying woman who was not then of sound mind, and was subjected to the undue influence of the Rev. Alured Black and his wife.

A "special jury" was empanelled to hear the case before Mr. Justice Gorell Barnes, of the Court of Probate, Divorce and Admiralty on 14 November 1895. Most Britons would likely have thought that the disinherited Clelands certainly had reason to be suspicious. As the end closes in, a clergyman will often have unique access to the bedside of the testatrix, as we must now know Miss Anne. Therefore, when a will benefits a clergyman – as this will clearly did, courts will observe with "the same jealousy of fraud and imposition." Still, the claim of "undue influence" was not one so easily proven.

The Rev. and Mrs. Black were represented by Mr. John Murphy, QC. Dublin born and educated, Murphy would be the man who would have to defend the last will to be written by the late spinster from County Down. The Irish brogue was to be the dominant voice in the three days the case occupied in the Royal Courts of Justice in London. Said to be the heaviest barrister in Britain (and his *Vanity Fair* caricature is evidence in support of that dubious honour), it was also said of Murphy: "If a ballot of the profession were taken it would probably be found that he is also the most popular." Murphy began with a lengthy statement recapitulating the events of the previous twelve years, beginning with the late Miss Anne Cleland's written pledge to Col. George Black that she intended to leave her niece independent. That wish was encompassed in the will of 1885. Murphy insisted that the Rev. and Mrs. Black never had any inkling that Miss Anne had changed that will until March of 1893. More than a year before Miss Anne's death, when she was still in good health and of a sound mind, she had asked to see a solicitor for she wished to write a new will, re-establishing her intention to leave everything to Annie. Mr. Coaks, a Norwich solicitor of some standing, was consulted and having received a letter of instruction from Miss Cleland, a new will was drawn up. Mr. Coaks, accompanied by his partner and a clerk as witnesses, took the new will out to Buxton rectory where the document was signed by Miss Anne

Cleland on 22 March 1893. This was all quite appropriate and above board. Murphy declared that the charges of undue influence made against the Blacks were outrageous and false.

First, the Rev. Black, and then, Mrs. Black, took the stand to deny there was any such plot to coerce their beloved relation into changing her will in their favour. Mr. Black swore that until Miss Anne had asked to see a solicitor, he was completely unaware of the 1888 will. He had assumed that the 1885 will was still in effect. Whatever, the subject was not one that he had discussed with Miss Anne since she had come to Buxton rectory in 1891. He insisted that Aunt Anne, at the time of her final will, was quite competent and not subject to any pressures from himself or his wife. Mrs. Black gave similar testimony. Under cross-examination, Mrs. Black was asked about her aunt's mental state while in Buxton. The rector's wife admitted that in January 1893, two months before the will had been changed, she had written to her sister and described Miss Anne as "doting." The clergyman's wife said that the word was not meant to imply that her aunt was incapable or of unsound mind, in any way. She was, simply, an old woman nearly 75 years old.

Dr. Samuel Barton of Norwich, who had treated Miss Anne Cleland during her final illness said that, at the time of the new will, the woman had been of clear intellect and was quite capable of acting for herself. She had been very kindly treated by the Blacks in her final illness and he saw no signs of any imposition on the part of the rector or his wife.

Isaac Bugg Coaks – who some years before had his name legally changed to add the (somewhat) more euphonious Coaks bit – explained his role in preparing the will signed by Miss Cleland. He admitted that the Rev. Mr. Black had come to him in March 1893 to ask that he make a trip out to Buxton rectory. Coaks said he could not do that without an express written request from Miss Cleland herself, which was soon forthcoming. He then did travel to the rectory, where he met privately with Miss Anne. She instructed him to re-write the will as written in 1885. She seemed to be completely capable of making that decision. He saw no evidence that she was being coerced in any way. Her instructions were carried out and the new will witnessed and signed as required by law.

William Willis, brogue free, was the counsel for James Cleland and Florence Stirling. In addition to his duties at the bar, he was an MP. In the House of Commons, he once spoke so passionately that he crushed the hat of the "right honourable friend" seated in front of him. In a court-room, however, it was said, "He can roar as softly as any sucking-dove and is excellent in managing a timid witness." Mr. Willis informed the jury that the 1885 will was not the first will ever written by Miss Anne Cleland. As far back as 1872, she had written a will – produced in evidence - that stated her full intention to divide her property equally amongst her two nieces – Annie & Florence. It is interesting, Willis suggested to the jury, that both the 1885 will and this newly proffered will of 1893, had been written by Miss Cleland during a time she was staying under the roof of and, it must be charged, under the influence of the Rev. Mr. Black. Willis said that Miss Anne's laudable promise, given to the late Col. Black, that she intended to leave her "independent," could not be stretched to imply that she meant to leave her everything. Further, could the Rev. Mr. Black be believed when he said he was not aware that Miss Cleland had changed her will, lessening the portion due to his wife? The rector's active role in the preparation of a new will would indicate he was well aware of how the ground had changed since 1885. In sum, Willis argued, the will of 1893, had been prepared under "undue influence" and could not represent the true last wishes of Miss Anne Cleland.

The first two witnesses on behalf of the Cleland claimants were nurses who had worked at Buxton rectory during Miss Anne's final illness. A Miss Holden told the court that she had observed a distinct failing in the patient's mental faculties. She testified that it was her opinion that the woman was incapable of transacting any business of such importance. A second nurse, Miss Newsome entered the witness box to swear to similar conclusions. She also testified that she had observed that the required letter written by Miss Anne to Coaks, the solicitor, asking the latter to come out to the rectory, had been copied from a letter written out first by the Rev. Black. The vicar had told Miss Anne that it was just a formality and she would have to copy it out in her own hand. Miss Newsome also claimed to have been taken into the confidence of the dying woman who, at one point, said to her that Mr. Black was trying to get her to change her will. Miss Anne told the nurse that she always wanted to divide her fortune equally between her nieces. The old woman had also confessed to her nurse that she didn't like England at all and she wished that she could just sit on top of a pile and slide down it and come out in Ireland. While Nurse Newsome's evidence amused the courtroom quite a bit, such hearsay deathbed testimony is much frowned upon as a rule. Miss Anne, of course, was now beyond the reach of the counsel for the other side.

Nevertheless, despite the legal quibbles, Miss Newsome had put the suggestion of undue influence before the jury. Mr. Murphy, during his chance to question the young woman, showed her a statement that she had earlier signed, agreeing that Miss Anne Cleland was perfectly sane and not at all weak in the mind. Miss Newsome couldn't deny signing the paper but she said it only reflected her opinion at that particular time. She had since then reconsidered the point. The nurse said that it would be more accurate for her to have said that Miss Anne was "sometimes sane."

Mrs. Florence Stirling, the sister of Mrs. Black, said that by the will of 1893, she went from inheriting half her aunt's fortune to receiving nothing. Florence insisted that her aunt had often told her that she had very much regretted the decision in 1885 to make that original change in her will. In 1888, when she re-did the will, Miss Anne had told Florence it had always been her wish that the sisters would divide her property. Florence also presented letters from Buxton rectory in which her sister suggested that Miss Anne was failing. These letters pre-dated the time the new will was drawn up.

James Cleland was an interesting figure in the whole controversy over his aunt's estate. It had always been Miss Anne's intention to split her estate only between his two sisters. He had the income from the family lands in Crossgar. In 1889, during a slump in the rents, he had become seriously in arrears. At that time, his aunt agreed, in a codicil, that she would forgive him a mortgage debt of £1900. At her death, he was to be left clear of all claims on that mortgage. The new will, of course, contained no such provision. He was facing significant costs as a result of the new will. James told the court that his aunt had always relied on her brother-in-law, James Warnock, now deceased, to handle her legal affairs. When Warnock drew up the will in 1888, restoring the division between Annie and Florence, the solicitor then told Miss Anne that when she returned to England she must never show it to the Rev. Black lest he would put it in the fire. James said that none of the Irish Clelands trusted the Rev. Black; adding that it was impossible for him to accept that the rector was unaware of the changed fortunes of his wife's estate. Once he had the aging Miss Anne back under his roof, James said he knew the clergyman would not rest until he had the will changed once again.

Following the closing arguments from the two leading counsel, the jury was to hear the instructions of Justice Gorell Barnes. He had been just over two years on the court that dealt with the unlikely triad of Probate, Divorce and Admiralty cases. He was later celebrated for remarking that the women in Divorce Court wear too much perfume. Still, he found it diffi-cult dealing with the personal tensions in Probate and Divorce cases:

If I were to think over all the suffering and anxiety of all those poor people tonight I should wear myself out. I have schooled myself to look on them all as "cases" and very sad cases most of them are.

His Lordship explained that the jurors had two issues to decide: firstly, was Miss Anne Cleland of sound mind when she made out the will of March 1893? Secondly, was that will which benefited only Mrs. Annie Black (and, of course, her husband) obtained via the "undue influence" of the rector of Buxton and his wife? The simple fact that Miss Anne Cleland had changed and re-changed her will was no proof of her being under any "undue" influence. The disappointment experienced by James and Florence is not proof of anything. Mere change of intention is never enough; it must be coupled with evidence that she was being coerced. Coercion is a strong word. It does not require a whip and a chair. You can be coerced as much by sweetness and lies as by the harshest tones. The standard definition of coercion had been given in the Wingrove case of 1885 – and not with complete success:

> In may be in the grossest form, such as actual confinement or violence, or a person in the last days or hours of life may have become so weak and feeble that very little amount of pressure will be sufficient to bring about the desired result, and it may even be that the mere talking to him at that stage of illness and pressing something upon him may so fatigue the brain that the sick person may be induced, for quietness' sake, to do anything. This would equally be coercion, though not actual violence.

The jurors returned after two hours to report that they were still unclear on the law. His Lordship again explained that persuasion or inducement is not coercion. The testatrix may be led to make changes in her will but unless it can be proven that she was "driven to it," the claim of undue influence must fail.

The jurors returned a very short while later with their decision. There had been no under influence on the part of the Rev. and Mrs. Black. The jury found no reason to believe the dying woman – at the time the will was being written and signed – was of any diminished capacity. The will had been properly prepared and executed.

Before the Blacks could return to their Norfolk rectory, James Cleland filed a request asking the unstated costs of the lawsuit be deducted from Aunt Anne's estate. Justice Gorell Barnes harrumphed his reply in the negative. He said that a very serious charge had been brought against the Blacks and though argued "with vigour" by Mr. Willis, the charge had proven to be "without the slightest foundation." It is not good public policy to encourage such legal actions with the prospect of – win or lose – the costs will be covered out the estate. Request denied.

The Rev. and Mrs. Black had many years to enjoy their inheritance. He remained at Buxton until 1907. He was later vicar of Silsoe in Bedfordshire, resigning in 1931. He died four years later.

The Late Strange Circumstance at Letheringsett

Rev. William Browne, Rector of Letheringsett

ON A SUNDAY morning in September 1855, the Rev. William Browne was going about his Lord's business. He was to conduct services at St. Andrew's, the 12th Century parish church of the small village of Letheringsett, where he had been rector since 1852. St. Andrew's stands on the banks of the Glaven, a small stream that "pursues a very circuitous course" through the village and on then short distance to the North Sea at Cley. It is a beautiful setting and Letheringsett is fairly described as "one of the prettiest villages in Norfolk." A most extraordinary drama was about to unfold.

On that 16th of September, shortly after eleven, a gentleman carrying a small carpet bag came into the churchyard, having walked over from Holt, less than two miles to the southeast. Finding a man in the churchyard, the stranger came forward to inquire if this was indeed the church where the Rev. Mr. William Browne was rector. He was assured that he had found the right place. He asked if Mr. Browne was to be officiating on this Sabbath day. "None other than he," the visitor was again assured. The inquisitive man then asked if there might be a side door or a rear entrance to St. Andrew's church. The helpful villager said that, alas, the only entrance to the church was through the south porch and he directed him thither. Tipping his hat to his well-informed companion, the gentleman with the carpet bag turned and walked the short distance to the church door. But no sooner did he enter St. Andrew's, the visitor was wrestled to the ground. For you should know that the helpful man in the churchyard was no ordinary lurking local but rather no less a personage than doughty George Lambley, the Superintendent of Police from Holt.

Supt. Lambley's assistance had been sought by the Rev. Mr. Browne after a series of threatening letters. The author of those threats had vowed not to rest until the old clergyman had "swallowed a pistol ball." The man who was nicked in the church doorway was identified as Joseph Berridge. He was a man of nearly seventy years. Though he insisted to Supt. Lambley that he meant no harm to anyone, four percussion caps for a minie-pistol were found in one of his pockets. But he was carrying no gun. When his carpet bag was opened, Berridge cried out, "There's been a mistake, this isn't my bag!" The bag he had been toting contained only some clothing but no weapon. He was taken to the Holt jail to await a magistrate's court appearance on a charge of "feloniously sending a letter to the Rev. Mr. William Browne threatening to kill and murder him."

The rector of Letheringsett was sixty years old. He had never married. He was the eldest son of an Oxford don and had taken his own degree at Worcester College in 1816. After several itinerant years as a clergyman, Mr. Browne was invited by a friend to help establish the Cheam School in Surrey. He spent several years in Cheam and whilst there made the acquaintance of Joseph Berridge, who was then employed as the secretary of the Freemasons & General Life Assurance, Loan, Annuity and Reversionary Interest Company. Whew! Berridge resided in St. Swithin's in the City. Berridge had also been unmarried until the age of fifty; in 1838, he was married in Shoreditch to Mary Ann Doubell, a young woman from his home county of Leicestershire. The Berridges soon started their family: a first child, a son named George, was born in 1839 and their daughter Emily was born the following year. Eventually, there would be four Berridge children.

The intimacy between the Rev. Mr. Browne and the Berridges had continued until, in the 1840's, the clergyman left Cheam to take a family curacy at Elsing, near Dereham, in Norfolk. Whether from distance or dispute, correspondence between the former friends came to an end. In 1852, Mr. Browne arrived in Letheringsett to take up his new living. The letters began soon thereafter.

As for Berridge, it seems that he lost his job with the Freemason's in 1850. He may have been a casualty of the firm's rapid expansion – certainly a scenario not unfamiliar in today's City. The Freemason's was expanding rapidly, gobbling up several other firms and in 1849, it was renamed The Albert Life Assurance Company. Berridge would not be part of the firm going forward (nor he would he be around when "The Albert" collapsed in 1869 with losses of a then inconceivable £4,000,000). In 1852, the same year his former friend began his new life as rector, Berridge was making his living as a "Translator of several of the principal languages of Europe."

The background facts as known having been provided, we can return our attentions to the unseemly disturbance at the rear of Letheringsett church. Joseph Berridge was brought up before the magistrate the following morning. William Hardy Cozens- Hardy was a wealthy brewer and the occupant of Letheringsett Hall, not but a few yards from the church. However Cozens-Hardy was not one of the Rev. Browne's parishioners for he was a Methodist and one of the very few – if not the only - nonconformist magistrates in Norfolk at the time. The proceedings opened with the Rev. Mr. Browne explaining that his erstwhile friend had formed "the extraordinary delusion" that he was the father of one or more of the Berridge children. The rector insisted that there was absolutely no foundation for Mr. Berridge's belief, nor was their even the slightest reason to suspect any improper intimacy had ever existed between himself and Mrs. Berridge. He had repeatedly assured Berridge of these facts but nothing seemed to dissuade his tormentor and when the accusations advanced to threats of murder and violence, including a vow to shoot him dead in the pulpit, he felt that he had no recourse but to seek the assistance of the police.

Supt. Lambley said that he had asked the authorities in Norwich to put a watch on the trains coming from London into Norwich. He received word that a man matching Mr. Berridge's description had arrived on that previous Saturday. Berridge had then taken a coach from the Norfolk Hotel in Norwich to The Feathers, the inn in the market place at Holt where he had spent the night. This intelligence was all reported to Lambley. On Sunday, as we know, Mr. Berridge had walked in to Letheringsett. In plain-clothes, Lambley was waiting upon his arrival in the churchyard. The policeman recounted the series of questions that had been put to him by Mr. Berridge. He described the man as having conducted himself in a "highly excitable state." When Berridge finally attempted to enter St. Andrew's by the south porch, Lambley told the magistrate that he grabbed the man and placed him under arrest. Berridge had then told him that he had come to Letheringsett to give Mr. Browne "all he wanted" but he had insisted that he meant to do no injury to the clergyman. He was carrying percussion caps in his jacket pocket; however, there was no gun on his person or in the bag. When Lambley opened the carpet bag that Berridge was carrying, incredibly, it was soon established that it wasn't Berridge's bag at all. There had been a cock-up with the bags in Norwich. The coaching hotel had sent the wrong bag to The Feathers. In the interim, Berridge's actual bag had been finally located, and Lambley told the magistrates that it did contain a fully loaded minie-pistol.

The next witness was Barstead, a servant at The Feathers. When Berridge had arrived at the inn, Barstead had asked him why his bags had no identification on them. He said he was told by the visitor, "I am here on unpleasant business and I don't wish to have my name on the bag."

Mr. Hardy had heard enough and ordered that Joseph Berridge be held over for trial at the coming assizes. The brief session was crowded, with news of "the strange circumstance at Letheringsett" having quickly spread throughout the county. The magistrate said that he knew he spoke for all in the village in stating his belief that the charge made by this half-mad gentleman against the respected Rev. Browne could not be believed. Hardy also offered a generous word or two for Supt. Lambley whose canny management of the case had no doubt prevented a most horrific tragedy. (The good copper would soon rise to command the entire Swaffham division!)

Mr. Justice Erle was to hear the case against Joseph Berridge. The Old Bailey legend, Serjeant William Ballentine, appeared to prosecute the case, acting on behalf of the Rev. Mr. Browne. Ballentine stated that the accused gentleman had been tormenting the Rev. Browne for several years. Firstly, he accused the rector of Letheringsett of fathering some or all the Berridge children. With the rector's full co-operation and the assistance of many concerned friends of Mr. Berridge, the latter was – for a while anyway – convinced that he had been in error. However, Ballentine said that Berridge had then conceived the notion that if Mr. Browne was not the seducer of Mrs. Berridge, the rector knew who was. The threatening letters continued, now with new demands that Mr. Browne identify this "third man" in the frame. A typical letter was dated 14 July 1855:

> May God eternally damn you, you scoundrel. I will find you both someday and make you give me satisfaction so far as the affront is concerned, or swallow a pistol ball.

Ballentine said these threats had now been put into action. Though he was not carrying it with him that morning, Berridge had set out from London with a loaded pistol. The pistol was loaded with the new French-made Minie bullet, touted as having twice the range of its predecessors without losing any of its "destructive power." Ballentine reminded the court that only through the efforts of the local constabulary and the happenstance of the wrong bag having been sent along to Mr. Berridge's hotel in Holt, the murder of an innocent man might have occurred. Insisting that the rector of Letheringsett held not "the slightest vindictive feeling" for his former friend and his delusion, Ballentine said that Mr. Browne, however, had "no wish to die on account of that delusion." Until Mr. Berridge was placed under restraint, the Rev. Mr. Browne could not live in peace.

William Clarkson defended Berridge and insisted to the court that – other than on this particular subject – his client was a very competent gentleman, a man, in fact, of "great intelligence," who had held a responsible position in an important financial venture. Clarkson said that the most searching investigations had not turned up any evidence to link the Rev. Mr. Browne and Mrs. Berridge in any culpable activity. The defendant has been told this repeatedly by his many friends and it was to be hoped that he would now accept this as the truth. Regardless, a man now nearly seventy, Mr. Berridge, said Clarkson, was hardly a threat to anyone. The bag mix-up was almost comical. Would any serious assassin have gone off to murder someone and not checked to make sure he had the weapon with him? Clarkson told the court that Mr. Berridge keenly regretted his actions and his many friends would assure the court that this harassment of the blameless Rev. Mr. Browne would come to an end.

After seeing that the friends of the defendant were willing to post the hefty financial sureties to supervise his conduct, Justice Erle agreed to release Mr. Berridge. Addressing the defendant, Erle said he considered him "more diseased than guilty." But he sternly warned Berridge that he must "strive to overcome the miserable delusion under which you are labouring and not allow your neighbours or the world to see or hear any more of it." According to *The Morning Chronicle*, Berridge then attempted to make a statement that began by way of some explanation for the grounds of his beliefs. Justice Erle cut him off, "Say no more, I said." Berridge left the court a free man.

The Lancet thought Erle's ruling was highly irregular:

> We sincerely hope, for the clergyman's sake, that this admonition will have a curative effect; and if it should, it will then become a question calling for the most serious consideration, whether Mr. Justice Erle should not receive Her Majesty's commission to visit all the lunatic asylums, to administer judicial exhortations to madmen to give up their delusions – in short, to order them to cure themselves, and on the strength of their assurances and recognizances to discharge them! But we fear that it may happen that this admonition may not prove curative, and the next intimation of the persistence of the defendant's delusion may be the homicide of its object.

In fact, Mr. Berridge left the Old Bailey on 26 November 1855. Less than six weeks later, on 7 January 1856, Mr. Ballentine was back in Recorder's Court to claim that the Rev. Browne had received new threats against his life. Berridge had, meantime, opened a second front, sending hostile letters also to Mr. Cozens-Hardy, the Letheringsett magistrate. *The Times* thought the case had now taken on "a very extraordinary character." The situation was now clearly intolerable. How could this be? He had given his word; his friends had vouched for his future conduct. At first delusional, Mr. Berridge had become what the medical men had newly labeled a "monomaniac":

> He does not merely think about it erroneously, but it is ever present to his mind: talking, he speaks of it; silent, he thinks of it; sleeping, he dreams of it.

Earlier in the decade, Dr. J.C. Badeley of Cambridge had written that such individuals may appear to be perfectly sane and will declare their intent to reform, however, "The attempt at concealment is only to be witnessed in cunning monomaniacs, who have become aware that they are deemed insane." He predicted "great judicial difficulties."

The new and equally threatening letters from Berridge to the Rev. Mr. Browne were presented to the Recorder. Mr. Ballentine conceded that while it might be true that Berridge is mad on only this one subject, he could not be permitted to remain at large when he continues to threaten violence against Mr. Browne and others. It was to be regretted that the humane course taken by Mr. Justice Erle had not had its desired effect; therefore, Ballentine pleaded that the court immediately order that Berridge be taken into custody. The Recorder, Mr. Wortley, agreed and Berridge was ordered detained. Shortly thereafter, Mr. Justice Erle, this time without comment or exhortation, directed that Mr. Berridge be kept in Newgate jail for a period of not less than eighteen months. It was ordered that "every facility" be made available to the friends and physicians of this unfortunately deranged gentleman.

Dr. Robert Semple, one of Britain's leading practitioners of the fledgling science of psychiatry, said the failed efforts of Justice Erle in the Letheringsett case should be a lesson to those who display what he called "a morbid feeling" to allow liberty to anyone, even at the risk of others.

> The present state of the law is culpably lax ... where a man entertaining a *groundless* suspicion as to the virtue of his wife, utters a series of menaces against the *supposed* adulterer, and follows up his threats by an actual attempt (happily aborted) to destroy an innocent man. If the latter *had* been destroyed, the assassin would, of course, have been acquitted on the ground of insanity; and yet, because he has not *succeeded* in his murderous attempt, he is allowed to go loose upon his verbal promise —- the promise of a lunatic!

Mr. Berridge did not long survive his jail term. He died in London in September 1860. His traducer, real or imagined, the Rev. Mr. Browne outlived him, but only just. The rector died (it seems quietly) at his brother Henry's home in Worthing in May of 1861. He is buried in Letheringsett churchyard.

He Must Have Been a Driveling Libertine

The Rev. Lambert Blackwell Foster

THE REV. Lambert Blackwell Foster bore a name of some historic significance in Norwich. A century and a quarter before our story, a Sir Lambert Blackwell was one of the directors of the infamous South Sea Bubble. The Blackwells somehow survived that calamity with their wealth intact. In the years since, through marriage, the Blackwells had mixed with the Fosters, a family of bankers, solicitors and baronets in the cathedral city. In 1795, one of those baronets gave birth to a son, Lambert Blackwell Foster. Lambert would later enter the church. He held a small living in the Norfolk village of Brundall on the Yare. He came into a goodly fortune from an uncle Blackwell. He married a clergyman's daughter, raised a small family and spent much of his time at his "neat villa" in Brundall studying birds. He died in March of 1863.

You are no doubt asking why the Rev. Lambert Blackwell Foster has been consigned to this collection of clerical worthies. The answer is that for almost the entire last decade of his life, he lived with his mistress, a former (and occasionally practicing) prostitute. Moreover, the circumstances of their meeting were certainly unique. In 1852, one could, no doubt, have made a lengthy list of places in Norwich where an interested gentleman could find "a bit of what he fancies." It is extremely unlikely that Norwich Cathedral was on any such list.

As mentioned, the Rev. Mr. Foster was a married man. In 1821, he married Mary, a daughter of the Rev. Richard E. Browne, rector of Elsing, near Dereham. They had five children, two sons and three daughters. Alas, the Fosters were not happily married and they had separated as long ago as 1832. He no longer had a church or benefice and was listed on the rolls for the rest of his life as a "clergyman without cure of souls." He remained at Brundall with his birds and the family lived in Norwich. Mr. Foster was often in the city to visit his children and to see his brother, Sir William Foster, a prominent solicitor. The two brothers were very close and the baronet seems to have supported the clergyman throughout.

On 7 May 1852, the Rev. Mr. Foster was moved to pay a visit to Norwich Cathedral. There was nothing out of the ordinary in that, of course. The same day, the historic cathedral doors were also opened to Emma Baxter, a glazier's daughter from the village of Long Stratton who had been in service but had found that life, shall we say, less rewarding. At 18, Emma was probably no better than she had to be. It was a Friday. Perhaps the clergyman, perhaps Emma, or perchance both, came to this beautiful house of worship that day for spiritual consolation. A moment of individual prayer for the strength to face the differing challenges and travails ahead. Regardless, they left together. The 57-year old clergyman was completely taken with this flirty young lady. If not that very day, then very soon, they met again at "one of those discreditable places" in Norwich that offered a room for certain purposes.

The besotted Rev. Mr. Foster knew that he could not cavort in the streets of Norwich with this woman. The city was too crowded, with his estranged wife, his respected brother, and dozens of people who would know him on sight. With the delightful Emma in tow, Foster thusly went off to London where he took a lease on a home at 7 Upper Belgrave Street. He told the giddy girl that she had a free hand and his purse to furnish the place. They settled in to live there as man and wife.

Oh, it was not going to be easy. There were quarrels. Mr. Foster was quite particular about his meals and his rest. Young Emma had a bit more "energy" about her than did her new protector. On one occasion, after a spat, Foster dozed off. He awakened to find his songbird had flown. For more than a week, he searched everywhere. He finally located a cabman who said he had picked up a young woman in Belgravia that evening. He had taken her to Oxenden Street. The Rev. Mr. Foster must have been furious when he discovered the address was another of those "discreditable places." Waiting outside for hours, he saw her at last. Racing up to her, he dropped to his knees to beg her forgiveness for his ill-temper and to plead with her to come back with him to Upper Belgrave Street. She agreed. He also invited her mother to come there from Stockwell and her younger sister also joined the menagerie.

Life went back to – what passed for – ordinary at Upper Belgrave Street. On 7 May 1853, which date Mr. Foster would forever call "their anniversary," he showered her with jewellery. More would follow. He told Emma that his wife and children despised him, and the jewellery should be hers, "No one will appreciate all of this as much as you." Not jewels alone did he lay at her feet. His brother, Sir William, came to dine. He recognized the family plate and Emma chirpily told him, "This is all to be mine some day." Rev. Mr. Foster echoed her words, "Oh, yes. Yes."

They remained in Belgravia almost three years. Whether to avoid the city crowds, noise and odors, or simply to get his susceptible "little darling" away from the city's dangerous allures, in 1855 Rev. Foster announced they were moving to the country. He told Emma to pack up all the furniture, plate, jewels etc and off they went to East Anglia.

Their new home was Fritton Old Hall in the village of Fritton, which sits on Fritton Lake or Fritton Decoy and, it has been said, "there can be no doubt it is the gem of Norfolk scenery." Until the county border was redrawn in the 1970's, the village of Fritton was actually in Suffolk. However beautiful the setting of her new home, Emma found the transition from fashionable West End London to this remote place a very taxing matter. She soon chose to run away again. It seems some of the female servants were even less delighted with the move and they prevailed upon Emma to make a bolt with them for the bright lights of Yarmouth. The Rev. Foster found the trail very easy to follow and was soon in Yarmouth to again gather up his "wife," and no doubt abandon the faithless help. Emma, however, was proving to be increasingly difficult. She next bolted to her mother, who had opted out of the move to this rustic retreat and had returned to Stockwell. This new skip job was of some greater concern to Foster because Emma had taken all of the jewels with her. Bringing the recalcitrant Emma back to Fritton, he then told her that the jewels would be safer in the bank. By taking them out of the house, she might well have lost them (or sold them?) She shouldn't worry, though, because he had made a will leaving everything to her. The jewels were secured at Harvey & Hudson's Bank in Norwich.

In the census of 1861, the Rev. Foster made no effort to hide his situation. He was registered as a married clergyman, without cure of souls. His wife was not living with him. There were four servants at Fritton Hall, a cook, a housemaid, a coachman and a groom. Also registered as a "visitor" at the Hall was Emma Harriett Baxter, age 27, and in the (unusually) bold and clear hand of the census taker, Emma was described as "an independent lady." Emma's sister Clara, a year younger, was also registered as a "visitor" in Fritton.

In March of 1863, the Rev. Lambert Blackwell Foster died at Fritton Hall. His eldest son, 38 year old William Foster, [not to be confused with his namesake uncle, the baronet] soon descended upon Fritton with orders for Miss Emma Baxter to vacate at once and not take a thing with her besides her personal effects and clothing. The jewellery, the china, the plate, the furniture was all Foster property. She was offered £300 for her years as "a companion" to his father in his dotage. She could deduct from that any needed cartage fees for her sister and their bag and baggage. But, bottom line, she must go. Emma was in a difficult position. In the days after the Rev. Foster's death, she, her sister, and even *Sir William* Foster, had ripped apart Fritton Old Hall but found no will. Nothing turned up at the bank, either. Despite his promise to Emma, the old reprobate had died intestate. She would have to fight for what she believed was hers.

In August of 1863, before Mr. Justice Wightman and a jury at the Ipswich Assizes, Emma Baxter filed suit against William Foster, the eldest son of the Rev. Mr. Foster, and the family's protagonist. Mary Foster, the clergyman's wife survived him but seems to have remained discreetly out of the way. Emma's lawsuit, in the ancient argot of the law, was an action of *detinue sur trover*. She was claiming that she had the greater right to the "chattels" of Fritton Old Hall – the plate, the furniture and her promised jewels – than did any of the Fosters who had "detained them" since the old man's death. Emma's lawyer was Peter Frederick O'Malley, recorder of Norwich and the leading barrister on the circuit.

The most important witness would be, of course, Emma herself. The newspapers reported that she was "tall and very good-looking and dressed in the most fashionable mourning." She, more than once, showed signs of emotion during her testimony. O'Malley led her through the story of her first meeting with the Rev. Mr. Foster in Norwich Cathedral. He was a very lonely and unhappy man and their relationship brought him new life. When she first learned he was a married man, her mother told her to leave him straightaway but she would not do that to him. They soon considered themselves to be husband and wife. She presented a book that had been inscribed by each of them in turn: "Emma Foster from her affectionate husband. Lambert Foster from his affectionate wife."

When Mr. Foster decided they should live together in London, he took a house and he told her to furnish it. She had selected everything. When they later moved to Fritton, he wrote her a note: "My Darling Emma, we are going to the country, take whatever furniture you like." She was always told to think of it as "her furniture." As for the china and the plate, Rev. Foster had brought that into the house, but, more than once, he had said it was also to be hers. Most of it had come from Brundall and she presented a list that Mr. Foster had drawn up of each item. He had given her that list.

The most expensive of her claims was for the jewellery, variously estimated to be worth several thousands of pounds. On their first "anniversary," she said that her lover first gave her jewellery, specifically a gold chain and drop, a gold necklace and two gold bracelets. More such presents followed and he had given her jewels every "anniversary" including their last in May of 1862. He had promised that it would be hers to keep as "no one in his family would care for it as much as me." She said the jewels were kept in a japanned tin at Harvey & Hudson's and, in the witness box, she was able to describe the pieces from memory.

At his death, and here again, the lovely witness fought to control herself, she had fully expected there would be the promised will. No will had been found but she insisted that it was the oft-stated wish of her lover of more than ten years, that should she have all of these things.

Henry Mills QC was the barrister for the Foster family and it would be to him to challenge this romantic tale. He wanted to know if Miss Baxter, prior to the Cathedral connection, had been a prostitute. She replied, in what was reported to be a firm voice, "I lived at places not much to my credit but I did not walk the streets." She conceded that soon after meeting the Rev. Foster, they went to a house of assignation. At the time, she was eighteen. She knew he was very much older than herself. She knew he was a clergyman. She did not know, at first, that he was a married man living apart from his wife and children. She rejected her mother's advice not to get involved with the Rev. Foster.

Whilst in London, she admitted that she ran away from her benefactor and returned to her former life. She admitted that she had been living at a brothel in Oxenden Street. Emma said her flight had been prompted by an argument.

Q: What did you quarrel about?

A: He would have his puddings his own way. [Laughter]

Q: So you left him?

A: When he was fast asleep. For a week. Not that he was asleep for a week. [Laughter] I was gone for a week until he brought me back.

She said that when Rev. Foster found her in Oxenden Street, he went onto his knees to beg her to return and she agreed to do so.

When she ran away from Fritton to Yarmouth, with servant girls for her companions, what was her intention? Emma said she had been "over-persuaded" by the servants and was simply hoping to have some fun at the seaside. There were more arguments when she was once again returned to Fritton. She ran home to her mother and this time took the jewels with her. Why did she think that the Rev. Mr. Foster took the jewels away from her upon her return? Emma insisted that he was worried about a fire at the old Hall. Yet he put the jewels in Harvey & Hudson's bank under his own name and his alone. He had told her that this would create less confusion and "trouble" at the bank.

There were only two other witnesses. Clara Anne Baxter, Emma's younger sister, who – of course – supported all that her sister had stated. She had been present on many occasions when the Rev. Mr. Foster had made statements that such-and-such was to be Emma's. Sir William Foster, the younger brother of the late cleric, also swore to having been present when similar oral promises were made. As his brother's solicitor, however, he admitted that he had not been party to the draughting of any will. A search of Fritton Old Hall had turned up nothing.

Mr. O'Malley told the jury in closing that the Rev. Lambert Blackwell Foster had not been a happy man. There were, in fact, only two people in the world he cared for, his brother – Sir William – and the young woman in court, Emma Baxter. She had brightened the last decade of his life. He had frequently made it clear to her that she was to have those items he had purchased for her – the furniture and some of the jewellery – or presented to her – more jewels and the Foster family plate. At his death, there was no will. Enter the vengeful Fosters. William Foster, the official "defendant," very well knew that by his actions he would bring this shameful matter before the public. Did he hate his father that much? Was he willing to bring shame upon his mother? Rather than let this poor young woman, left without anything, have some plate & jewels, young

Foster would suffer the family's disgrace to be known across England. The family throughout had been actuated by the meanest of motives.

This was a callous attack on one of the leading families of Norfolk, blustered Mr. Mills in his response. When William Foster evicted Emma Baxter from Fritton Old Hall, he was merely carrying out the wishes of the family. Throughout he had acted on behalf of his injured mother and his brother and sister. What about the Rev. Foster's decision on three occasions to take this profligate woman back into his home? He did this even when he knew she had gone back to her former life. Were those the actions of a rational man? The family thinks not. Therefore, his wild "promises" cannot possibly be relied on. Mills told the jury to consider the absence of a will very carefully. It was their belief that - by making no will – the Rev. Mr. Foster was "intending to do a tardy act of justice to those who, by his immoral course of life, he had for so many years cruelly wronged."

Turning at last to sum up for the Ipswich jurymen, Justice Wightman urged that they not be swayed by the "romance" of the story:

> This is not the history of a young and innocent girl seduced by the arts of an older man, but that of a woman living away from her parents, and after a short interview with a gentleman, who ought to have acted in a better manner, going off to live with him as his wife but really as his avowed mistress. It is no case therefore to create a jury's sympathy.

Everyone had assumed there was a will. Of course, there was none to be found. Justice Wightman said that if the Rev. Mr. Foster knew that there was no will, it might explain his wish to so frequently make verbal promises that this or that would be Miss Baxter's in the end. It was very common for someone to verbally present jewellery, by simply stating, "I want this ring to be yours." However, for someone to pass on furniture or the family plate by word of mouth, Wightman thought that might be considered an "odd circumstance." It then, at bottom, was a very simple case. Who had the greater right to possess these items? Did the Rev. Mr. Foster intend for the jewels to be the property of Miss Baxter and, if so, what was their value? The same question must be asked about the furniture and about the china and plate.

The jurors found that the Rev. Foster had intended that his lover Emma Baxter should have the jewellery he had presented to her. They put a value on the jewels, however, at just £1000. If the Fosters wanted them back, that was the sum they would have to pay Miss Baxter. The furniture was also to be Emma's; the wardrobe, chiffonier, etc were valued at £500. However, the Foster family plate and china was to remain in the hands of the family.

Thus ended a scandalous trial that had shocked, and greatly amused, by equal amounts. *The Morning Herald* thought the details "too painful for repetition," despite giving the matter several columns of attention.

> The plaintiff in the witness box was confessedly a worldly, greedy, young woman; the elder Foster must have been a driveling libertine, who in his fatuity could forgive, and even coax her with presents, after she had returned to him from a week of infamy better suited to her character than Norwich cathedral.

The Fosters may have had their dishes back but at a cost of some public humiliation. Their cause had not been a popular one. The press even took to quoting Napoleon who reportedly had said, "Family scandals had better be forgotten, if at all possible, but in all events hidden at home." Mrs. Foster, the abandoned wife, remained in seclusion in Thorpe with an unmarried daughter until her death in 1870.

Not to range beyond our subject but the sad end of Emma Baxter must not pass without notice. Soon after the trial, she took a new lover, a Cambridge born barrister, legal writer and "sportsman," John George Witt. They lived as man and wife in and around London for 23 years. In both the 1871 and 1881 census, she is reported as his wife. They had never married. In October of 1887, she went to the Grosvenor Mansions in Victoria Street where he had rooms and threw herself from the roof. She was 53. According to the report of the inquest in *The Times*, Witt told the coroner that she had "taken to habits of intemperance." We cannot know but perhaps Witt had indicated that he wished to find a suitable wife. We do know that Witt was married the following summer.

For Emma Baxter Foster Witt it was a tragic end to a life of romance – after her own fashion - that began in, of all places, Norwich Cathedral.

A Very
Unpleasant Charge

The Rev. Samuel Haworth
Vicar of Salhouse

THE VENERABLE Archdeacon John Bedingfield Collyer had been vicar of the twinned Norfolk parishes of Wroxham-with-Salhouse since 1801. The old clergyman shuffled off this mortal coil on a Sunday, 29 March 1857. He was 80. Although the Archdeacon had opted to spend most of his time at his splendid country home, Hackford Hall in Reepham, he had constructed a new vicarage near the church of All Saints in Salhouse. In 1857, the Rev. Samuel Haworth, his successor, moved in.

Salhouse was sometimes spelled Salehouse, or occasionally Sallowes, but invariably pronounced *Sailers.* At the time, it was what the directories liked to describe as a "straggling village." This was not meant to be a complimentary term as it suggests that the community has somehow managed to grow carelessly. The homes of the local residents of Salhouse were clustered along Upper and Lower Streets. The isolated church of All Saints can be found from Lower Street, by taking Bell Lane, where there still stands a pub of that name. The lane runs to the north, passing Salhouse Hall on the left. It is the home of the Ward family. Only just before our story, the squire, Richard Ward, had spent a goodly amount of his handsome fortune embellishing the church. Just beyond the hall the squat tower of the church of All Saints comes into view, "near the summit of an acclivity." Some have speculated the church was built so far from Salhouse itself out of fear of the plague. In the 14th century, more than 60,000 residents of Norfolk died in the Black Plague. Yet, others think the site was chosen simply for the higher ground. Archdeacon Collyer's new vicarage (constructed in 1846 and where now stands the modern Lodge Hotel) is even that bit further north from the village. This new home of the Rev. Mr. Haworth and his wife, however, was thought by contemporary observers to be quite "neat."

The other village under the spiritual leadership of the Rev. Mr. Haworth was Wroxham, just three miles to the north of Salhouse. While Salhouse was "straggling," Wroxham was "picturesque," on the "bold acclivities" of the River Bure. This, of course, predated the summer crowds attracted by the development of Wroxham as one of the main tourist stops in the Broads. From Wroxham, the Broads are navigable all the way to the sea at Yarmouth. Wroxham Broad itself was among the prettiest of them all and, in the mid-19th century, the scene of "an annual regatta patronized by the leading gentry." The church of St. Mary's in Wroxham was on an eminence near the river, and had also been restored by the late Archdeacon. Worshippers entered through what Pevsner called a "glorious doorway." He had much less to say about Salhouse church beyond remarking on what he thought was an "oddly lopsided" nave.

Curiously, however, the vicars of Wroxham-with-Salhouse preferred to reside at the vicarage in Salhouse. Presumably the vicarage in Wroxham, near the river, was a cold, damp place in the winter. It was also hard by the new railway.

The Rev. Mr. Haworth had arrived in Salhouse at the age of 33. Like the village he had come to, his name was variantly spelled: Haworth, Howarth and even Hayward. He had been born in the Cumberland port city of Whitehaven. He attended St. John's College at Cambridge, leaving with a B.A. and having been ordained in 1848. His first church assignment was as the curate of Stalmine, a small village in Lancashire. On 4 June 1850, the young curate married Ellen Briscoe, a woman much older than he. Ellen was then 39 and twelve years his senior. The Haworths remained in Stalmine until 1857 when he received the appointment to be the new vicar of Salhouse. The 1861 census shows that the Rev. Samuel Haworth and his wife Ellen were living in the Vicarage House, along with Sarah Webster, their general servant.

Sarah was from Worstead, a village some ten miles from Salhouse, and "the original seat of the manufacture of worsted stuffs to which it gives its name." She was just fifteen when she first came into service with the Rev. and Mrs. Haworth soon after the new vicar took up his church. Within a matter of months, if Sarah's word can be believed, the maidservant was seduced by the vicar and became his mistress. This clandestine arrangement continued until, perhaps inevitably, Sarah told her lover that she feared that she was with child. It proved to be a false alarm but not before Mr. Haworth had dosed her with gin and "something from the chemist." Notwithstanding his successful ministrations, the vicar decided that Sarah would have to go from Salhouse.

Having closely survived this brush with scandal, Mr. Haworth continued with his duties. He would also, apparently, continue his extra-marital adventures. On the first Sunday of the month of September in 1865, the Rev. Mr. Haworth and his wife were walking home from All Saints church, the morning Sabbath services having been completed. Their erstwhile maidservant, Sarah Webster, met them in the road. She begged to be allowed to speak to the vicar about her mounting debts, bills that she reminded Mr. Haworth that he had promised to pay for her. Haworth sharply told her that it was a matter not fit for discussion on a Sunday and she must go away immediately. She threatened instead to go to the local magistrate. Haworth told her she might as well do as she pleased as he would have no more conversation with her. He then pushed her aside and called her a "worthless bitch."

The Haworths had not been home but a few minutes before Sarah was at the porch door ringing the bell. The Rev. Mr. Haworth rushed out of the vicarage, all but carrying Sarah down the path, until she fell or was pushed into a bush. Sarah would also make the claim that he had made sure he also got in a kick or two for good measure.

Such a tumult in the road, however isolated the church and vicarage in Salhouse might be, could not fail to draw interest and comment. The attentions of the local police were soon attracted to this flagrant breach of the peace. Sarah Webster was encouraged to bring charges against the vicar and he was, therefore, directed to appear before two local magistrates on 16 September 1865.

The Norwich papers headlined the case: *A Very Unpleasant Charge*. The Rev. Samuel Haworth answered the summons, accompanied by his wife, who would remain at his side throughout the shocking proceedings. He was to be charged with "an assault of a brutal character upon a young girl." Two local squires were to hear the case: Mr. John Longe of Spix-worth Hall and Lt Col John Stracey-Clitheroe JP of Sprowston Lodge. The prosecution was in the hands of John Carsey Chittock of Redwell Street, Norwich. Mr. Haworth's representative was Samuel Linay, managing clerk for William Sadd, a local solicitor. Mr. Chittock objected at first, saying that Linay was only a clerk and not a qualified practitioner but the magistrates agreed to allow the latter gentleman to participate.

Chittock called his first witness, Miss Sarah Webster, to be sworn. *The Norfolk Chronicle* described her as "delicate looking." She told the magistrates that she was now nearly twenty years old. Sarah had first come to Salhouse vicarage to be the general servant there when she fifteen. She had only been at the vicarage a few months when, in her words, she was first seduced by the Rev. Mr. Haworth. It happened in the garden. There were other occasions, as well. He had made vague promises to marry her, once his much older wife passed on. When she told him some weeks later that she feared she might be pregnant, he made her drink a mixture of gin, laudanum and some "black stuff" he had gotten from a chemist. It made her quite ill. Whether from a false alarm or the efficacy of the vile "medication," there had been no pregnancy. Regardless, Mr. Haworth had told her she had better find work elsewhere and he instructed her to give notice to her mistress that she would be gone at month's end. He would try to find her another place in service. She was at present living in Norwich with the Denmarks, a tailor and his wife.

In October of 1862, she had a chance meeting with the Rev. Mr. Haworth in the cathedral city. They had a friendly conversation during which he asked if she might like to meet some day "for a tea?" He made the arrangements at the White Hart Inn on St. Peter's Street. She kept the appointment and testified that Haworth had booked one of the hotel's private rooms. Once there, whether before or after tea cannot be known, he once again committed adultery with her. Apparently, Sarah provided a thorough narration of the events at the White Hart but *The Norfolk Chronicle* considered it all to be "unfit for publication." It probably does not require a great deal of imagination to fill in the blanks. This time, as it happened, she did become pregnant and gave birth to a child in July of the following year. Mr. Chittock asked her plainly, "Who was the father of that child?" She indicated that it was the defendant, the Rev. Mr. Haworth. The child was not healthy and the confinement had left her in a greatly weakened state as well. This required the regular medical attendance from a Dr. Allen. The vicar had at first agreed to pay all of her medical expenses.

Sarah conceded that Mr. Haworth had dutifully kept the pledge, but – apparently after the child died – he ceased paying any of *her* bills. The young woman claimed that her health had not recovered still and she was now in arrears to the doctor for her care in the sum of £20.

It was owing to the clergyman's repeated failure to make the payments that Sarah said she had determined to walk from Norwich to Salhouse on a Sunday to confront Mr. Haworth. She insisted she had not come all that way solely to make a scene and only came on a Sunday because she could be sure that he would be at home on that day. He roughly pushed her aside in the street and said he would not speak in public "to such a worth-less bitch as I was." She testified that she then threatened to go to Wroxham Hall, where resided Mr. R. Blake Humfrey, the Deputy Lord Lieutenant of Norfolk and a one-legged hero from Wellington's Peninsular campaign. Haworth told her she could do what she wished but if she dared come to the vicarage, he would have her charged by the police. In the end, she did not go to Mr. Humfrey's but, instead, she defiantly made her way to the vicarage. Sarah testified that when she rang the bell, the vicar "popped out" and he grabbed her by both arms and dragged her from his porch and threw her into some bushes at the end of the path and kicked her. She said the brutal treatment had left her with several bruises on her person and her dress had been badly torn. A dress, by the way, she told the magistrates that she proudly valued at ten shillings. She then walked back to Norwich, passing Mr. Haworth's curate in the road near Wroxham. Upon her return to her lodgings with the Denmarks, she collapsed.

Mr. Linay, the solicitor's clerk, was given his opportunity to question Miss Webster and attempted to establish that her version of the events of that Sunday in Salhouse was greatly overstated. Mrs. Haworth was with the reverend gentleman when Sarah approached them. Would a cler-gyman on a Sunday have used such words in the presence of his wife? Sarah insisted that she had recalled his words exactly. Had Mr. Haworth not warned her to keep away from the vicarage where she had no right of trespass? She had been so warned. As for the "brutal assault," Linay, by his questions, suggested that Sarah's fall had occurred when Mr. Haworth, in his justifiable efforts to remove her from his property, had stepped on the train of her dress. In the process, the dress had been torn. Sarah said that all she knew was that her dress had been ripped in the struggle, and Mr. Haworth was to blame. As for the reported kicks, Mr. Linay asserted that it was Mr. Haworth's habit to remove his boots in the hours between the Sunday morning and evening services and at the time of this unwanted visitor's intrusion, he was wearing only a pair of very light carpet slippers. Sarah Webster would not back down; she maintained that he was yet wearing his regular heavy boots. Sarah did admit, however, that Mrs. Haworth had very kindly brought her out a glass of water. The vicar's wife had also told her servant to allow Sarah to sit for a few minutes in the kitchen to regain her strength but then she must go away.

It would, perhaps, have been remiss on Linay's part, had he not made an effort to impugn the character of the Rev. Mr. Haworth's accuser. Whether she had or had not had carnal relations with the vicar of Salhouse was one thing. It could also be suggested, however, that she had been intimate with other male persons who might also have fathered her unfortunate child. Mr. Linay asked Sarah if she was familiar with a Mr. Ellis? She allowed as how she knew him, but only by sight. She said the same about a Mr. Slaughter, apparently a (well-named) butcher whose shop was near her current lodgings.

If Mr. Linay, as he took his seat, was well-pleased with his efforts, it would be a short-lived feeling. Mr. Chittock rose to re-examine Sarah. He began by raising again the issue of why she came out on a Sunday to confront Mr. Haworth.

> Q: Had she tried on any other day to get him to speak with her?
> A: I had once tried to confront him at a place where I could find him in Heigham. They would not open the door there.
> Q: Who lives there?
> A: Harriet Child, a woman who goes by the name of Miss Harbord.
> Q: Was he there when you went to him?
> A: Yes.
> Q: I suppose someone else lives in the house besides Miss Harbord?
> A: No, she lives alone.
> Q: Except when the defendant is there?
> A: Yes.
> Q: Did the person who lives in the house at Heigham ever live at Salhouse.
> A: No, she lived at Wroxham.
> Q: What was she at Wroxham?

A: She was the governess of the school there.
Q: When did you go to Heigham?
A: The week before I went to Salhouse.
Q: They would not let you in?
A: No, sir.

Mr. Linay, however tardily, objected to this line of questioning as irrelevant to the assault charge before the magistrates. Chittock, however, said that when his young (and inexperienced) friend raised the names of Messrs Ellis and Slaughter, it had opened the way for similar reflections upon the character of Mr. Haworth. The prosecutor told the magistrates, "I knew that would let in all of this." The magistrates agreed.

Only two more witnesses were to be heard for the prosecution. Mr. Haworth's own curate, the Rev. James Stewart Gordon Cranmer, who had taken the services in Wroxham on 3 September, was walking toward Salhouse, and saw Sarah Webster coming in the other direction. At first, he paid her no notice but she spoke to him and he became then aware that the "poor little girl's dress [was] nearly torn from her back." Mr. Cranmer obviously was unaware of what had happened in Salhouse but his first thought was that the young woman had been "inhumanely treated." She was in great distress and appeared exhausted. He walked with her some way but she then took the road to Norwich. Cranmer told Mr. Linay that while Sarah's dress was torn, he saw no bruises.

The final witness was Mrs. Denmark, the tailor's wife from New Catton in Norwich. She testified that Sarah returned late on the Sunday of 3 September in some distress. Her dress was torn and disarranged. There were bruises and other marks indicative of a struggle. Mrs. Denmark then produced the dress in question, prompting a scramble among the onlookers to catch a glimpse of the famous and now much bedraggled frock. Mrs. Denmark said she was well aware of Sarah's relationship with the Rev. Mr. Haworth; in fact, the clergyman had come to their home on at least one occasion to leave a sovereign for her young lodger. Mr. Linay asked the landlady if Miss Webster had any current means of employment? How, in fact, given her alleged poor health, was she paying her rent?

This would suggest the point that Miss Webster was perhaps in some less than honourable profession. Mrs. Denmark admitted that Sarah was frequently too unwell to work but she did occasionally earn her keep by doing some dressmaking.

It was now up to Mr. Linay to make the case for the vicar of Salhouse. He told the magistrates that he would have to speak for the Rev. Haworth as "his mouth was closed." Nor would the law allow the defendant's counsel to call Mrs. Haworth to testify, even though the vicar's wife was the only other person to have been present at both the meeting in the road and, later, the struggle on the vicarage porch. Linay insisted that he would do his best to show that the vicar had "simply used as much force, and no more, as was necessary to eject the complainant from his premises after she had been warned that if she came there she would be turned off." This, after all, he reminded the magistrates, was the right of any Englishman when confronted with a trespasser. Sarah had no right to come to the vicarage; she was no longer employed there. Let her go away and press her case by other means than by insulting the Rev. Haworth and his wife in a public street on a Sunday. She then dared come to his home regardless. In his justifiable wrath, the clergyman had admittedly pushed her from the porch and led her down the path. The woman's dress was undoubtedly torn. Linay said neither he nor the magistrates had any idea if that tattered dress shown in court had not been torn subsequent to the events of that Sunday, but, if not, it most likely had happened when the vicar stepped on the dress, thus causing the girl to fall in the bush.

Linay again stressed to the magistrates that this was a simple assault case and nothing more. Whatever might be the nature of the unfortunate relationship that Miss Webster claimed to have had with Mr. Haworth, it was none of the magistrates' business to inquire. However, since the magistrates, over his objections, had allowed these allegations to be placed on record, he could only do justice to his client by requesting that he be allowed to question the defendant under oath. He begged that, in fairness to Mr. Haworth, the clergyman be afforded the "opportunity of denying these assertions."

Both the prosecutor, Chittock, and G.E. Simpson, the magistrate's clerk, argued that such a procedure was "altogether illegal." Since Mr. Haworth had chosen to be represented by an attorney, he could not be heard as well. It was the law of evidence. Linay said he did not need to be told that his request was irregular but he made the plea because the case was such an extraordinary one and the outcome could have certain "momentous" implications for Mr. Haworth. The magistrates declined Linay's request and instructed him to get on with his case.

The only defense witness was Sarah Alexander, the current housekeeper at Salhouse vicarage. She was at home on that Sunday morning and heard the ring at the door. It was her custom to greet all guests but as she went to the door, the Rev. Haworth appeared and said he would handle it on this occasion. She was still standing there when he opened the door and confronted Sarah Webster. Miss Alexander (to keep the two Sarah's separate) said that the woman was very loud and Mr. Haworth took her by the arms and "pushed her up the walk." In the process, he stepped on Sarah's dress and it was torn. She then fell into a bush. Miss Alexander did not see the vicar kick her. In any event, the servant testified that Mr. Haworth had removed his boots and was wearing a pair of light carpet slippers. Miss Alexander recalled that her mistress, Mrs. Haworth, then came out to give the other Sarah some water and she told the new Sarah to bring the old Sarah into the kitchen for a few minutes to rest. Finally, the vicar came into the kitchen and ordered Sarah Webster to leave or the police would be called. Miss Alexander also testified that while Sarah was in the kitchen, she had a good chance to observe the torn dress. The servant said that she was certain that the dress shown in court must surely have been torn in some additional way after Sarah Webster had left the vicarage.

Mr. Chittock launched his questioning of this loyal servant girl by returning to the compelling question of the vicar's footwear that morning. Since Sarah Webster had directly followed the Rev. Mr. Haworth home to the vicarage and then rang the porch bell, how had he the time to go inside the vicarage, upstairs to his room, remove his boots and put on his carpet slippers, and, yet, he was back down stairs to answer the bell himself. Miss Alexander said that the vicar had come "racing" to the door in his slippers. The poor servant girl was also forced to admit that since she was standing behind the vicar for much of the time and since Miss Webster was such a very small woman, she might not have had the clearest view of how exactly Mr. Haworth had managed to "push her up the walk." Mr. Chittock dismissed the witness and suggested to the magistrates that Miss Alexander's testimony had merely supported the prosecution's case.

The courtroom was now cleared for the magistrates to be allowed the privacy to deliberate. It was not a very long time before the public was readmitted. The vicar of Salhouse was informed:

> Mr. Haworth, we have given this very disagreeable case every attention in our power; we have considered the evidence both for and against, and without the slightest hesitation we must convict you. It was, certainly, one of the grossest assaults that ever came before this, or any, court.

The assault itself, a matter of a few bruises and a torn dress, was not, in itself, a very aggravated one. However, the magistrate continued, the identity of the perpetrator and circumstances of the incident made the matter wholly disgraceful:

> One could hardly believe, if it had not been stated upon oath in a court of justice, that a gentleman – I ought not to say that – that a *person* in your position, a clergyman having performed his duty on a Sunday, and going to perform it a second time, should, in the interval, come in contact with this young woman and assault her as you did.

Whatever Mr. Linay may have stated as to the limited scope of this inquiry, it was obvious to all that beyond the courtroom, this was much more than a simple assault case.

> We have heard other very disagreeable, most painful and disgraceful allusions to what I may almost call facts, which certainly do not come before us and it is not our duty to dwell upon them in any way. But with regard to the assault it is proved without the slightest difficulty at all. Your own evidence does not avail you in any way.

The maximum penalty for the crime was £20 or six months in gaol but the magistrates opted to halve the fine. However, they also decreed that Mr. Haworth must cover all costs of the prosecution. If he was unable to pay, he would then have to serve a three month term. The magistrates reported that only because the statutes did not allow them to mandate hard labour would they not impose it. The Rev. Haworth was given but two hours to find the money and a policeman was instructed to remain with him at all times. He found the money to pay the fine within the allotted time. Had he used that money to pay Sarah Webster's medical bills, would any of this have happened? It would, perhaps, have merely been postponed. Whatever, Mr. Haworth was allowed to go free.

While Mr. Haworth was free, perhaps, of his civil penalties, the "momentous" implications that the vicar's counsel had feared were soon apparent. The Rev. John Thomas Pelham, the Bishop of Norwich, had already set the wheels of discipline in motion. Pending the result of that investigation, the Bishop had immediately suspended Mr. Haworth from "the exercise of his ministerial functions." By December, following a closed-door inquiry, a panel of Norfolk clergy had determined that there was "prima facie" evidence to send the facts of the Sarah Webster matter and "another case" to the Court of Arches. The other case, apparently, would involve the erstwhile governess of Wroxham school now "calling herself Miss Harbord" and residing in Heigham. In February 1866, the Rev. Samuel Haworth, vicar of Wroxham with Salhouse was suspended from all duties for a term of three years for "adultery and immorality."

Suspension, was that punishment enough? The radical newspapers were decidedly dissatisfied with the discipline meted out to this – mockingly titled – "muscular Christian." *Reynolds' Newspaper* noted that Mr. Haworth had been judged guilty of seduction, abortion, falsehood and brutality, but the faithful in Salhouse need only wait upon the return of "this pious and godly man." *The Era* was more direct: "It would be too monstrous if this man were ever again allowed to preach the religion he has defiled."

In whatever way the Rev. Mr. Haworth would spend the years of his suspension - it would not be with his wife. Mrs. Haworth, apparently, had had enough of his infidelity. In 1871, the census-takers found her living once again in her hometown of Neston in Cheshire with an older sister. Ten years later, the two women were still together, residing in a home for aged women.

Samuel Haworth was less easily traced. No Bishop, apparently, would ever again employ the former vicar of Salhouse. His name, however, continued to appear in *Crockford's Clerical Directory* until as late as 1892. This was despite the fact that, annually, Mr. Haworth was listed as "not having sent his returns." From 1893, his name no longer appears.

Not Right In His Mind

The Rev. Edmund Holmes,
Chaplain of Heigham Hall, Norwich

O N A JUNE day in 1852, Elizabeth Bunn returned to the Wymondham cottage where she lived with her husband, Robert, an agricultural labourer, and their five children. Entering the cottage, to her great horror, she found her 13-year old daughter, Phoebe, lying on a bed with the Rev. Mr. Edmund Holmes. The outraged Mrs. Bunn expelled the 53-year old clergyman from her home and then she marched off for the local constable. The policeman quickly located the Rev. Holmes and took him immediately before the local magistrate.

This case was surely to be a difficult one for the magistrate, William Cann, a Norwich banker who resided at Cawick, near Wymondham. The Holmes family was wealthy and quite well respected in the Norwich area. In the worst case, if Mr. Holmes could be convicted of raping the girl, he might well hang for it. That said, before launching any criminal proceedings, Magistrate Cann thought it best that he first contact the Rev. John Holmes, the accused man's eldest brother and head of the family. After consultation, Cann and Rev. John agreed that Rev. Edmund should be placed without delay under the care of Dr. W.P. Nichols, one of the proprietors of nearby Heigham Hall, a private asylum for lunatics. Nichols duly hastened to acquire the requisite certificates signed by two independent doctors, not associated with his institution. That took some time but it was successfully done and the Rev. Edmund Holmes, having been certified insane, was admitted to Heigham Hall on 12 June 1852.

All involved must then have reflected upon their work as successful: a very painful and disturbing incident had been handled speedily and with the utmost discretion. But had it been done legally? That issue would not arise until two years had passed, when the debate over the case even reached the House of Commons. Had an "opulent" family managed to manipulate the Lunacy Acts to rescue the Rev. Edmund Holmes "from the gripe of the law" for his awful assault on a poor farm-worker's daughter? The scandal was heightened – if that was possible - by a new and startling revelation: after a period of treatment lasting all of a mere *two months*, the Rev. Mr. Holmes had been pronounced cured and discharged as a patient. The clergyman had then been permitted to remain (hide out?) at Heigham Hall where he had graciously agreed to serve as chaplain – although he was restricted to the spiritual guidance of the male patients. The press quickly seized upon the details of the Holmes case: *The Examiner*, was typical in its criticism, suggesting that even the lunatics in the asylum would not have selected the Rev. Holmes to be their chaplain, "They were hardly mad enough for such an outrage against all decency and fitness." The operators of Heigham Hall found themselves the focus of a national outrage.

The Rev. Edmund Holmes was born in 1798, a younger son of the Rev. Thomas Holmes, who for many years had been the vicar of All Saints church in the Norfolk village of Woodton, near Bungay. In retirement, the Rev. Thomas moved his rather large family to the village of Brooke, only a few miles to the southeast of Norwich but then described as "one of the prettiest and most retired villages in the county." There he had purchased Brooke Hall, the estate of the Cooper family and where the legendary surgeon, Sir Astley Paston Cooper had been born. In 1830, the old hall of the Coopers was pulled down and a new one built to the design of William Wilkins, the celebrated (and much criticized) architect of the new National Gallery in London. The new Brooke Hall, a "handsome cemented mansion in the Grecian style" was surrounded by parkland featuring "judiciously arranged trees" and a "fine piece of water." The Rev. Thomas did not live to enjoy his new demesne; he died in 1832 at the age of 73. His eldest son, the Rev. John Holmes took up his inheritance and became the lord of the manor, owning near 3000 acres producing an annual income of the then quite handsome sum of over £4000.

Besides John, Edmund's other siblings had also achieved some success. George Holmes had entered the military, become an officer in the

Dragoons, and then retired to erect his own manor house in Brooke. George then eased himself into the customary role of the local squire-magistrate. Two of Edmund's sisters had made successful clerical marriages: Margaret married a Rev. Blakesley, a future Dean of Lincoln Cathedral, and Martha took the hand of a clerical baronet, the Rev. Sir. T.C. Miller of Froyle in Hampshire. Edmund, however, had never married. After leaving Corpus Christi College in Cambridge in 1821, he had spent thirty years as a simple country clergyman. Owing to his eccentricities, he had not been able to hold down a position anywhere for a good length of time. He was most often employed as a curate. As far back as 1838, he was working for the Rev. William Wayte Andrew, the vicar of Ketteringham, who had once described his curate as "neurotic." In 1852, the year our story begins, Edmund was assisting in the parish of Wymondham, living in a cottage owned by Robert Bunn, a farm labourer, and the latter's wife, Hannah, who kept house. Phoebe Bunn, the victim of the Rev. Mr. Holmes's assault, was their niece. The census records reveal plainly that Bunns abounded in the Wymondham of 1852.

When first told of the awful charge that faced his brother and, of course, being quite familiar with Edmund's "eccentricities," the Rev. John Holmes of Brooke Hall, quickly agreed to approach Dr. Nichols of Heigham Hall. William Peter Nichols and Joseph Watson had opened their asylum on the Old Palace Road, northwest of the city, in 1840. John Ferra Watson had since succeeded his father as co-proprietor of the facility with Dr. Nichols. According to a Norfolk guidebook of the time:

> Heigham Hall, situated a little distant from the city, is capable of receiving sixty patients. The Hall is most commodious and commanding, and the grounds are very extensive and excellently arranged.

The hall was strictly private, accepting paying patients only. The Holmes family was certainly not alone in wishing, if such a choice was forced upon them, that their kinsman find refuge in such a facility. "All medical men are aware that the relations and friends of patients in the middle classes of society entertain a strong prejudice against sending them to an asylum where paupers are admitted," noted a writer in an 1852 edition of *The Journal of Psychological Medicine & Mental Pathology*. The 1851 census reveals that in the year before the Rev. Mr. Holmes' arrival, the list of male patients at Heigham Hall included one clergyman, two surgeons, five farmers, three gentlemen, four merchants, a solicitor and a bank manager. For reasons of privacy, the census identified the patients only by their initials.

The Holmes incident happened at a time of much debate and reform in the way the mentally ill were to be treated in Britain. It was a conversation on many levels. There was the debate – which must be said to continue today - over the best and most humane methods of care. In the early Victorian years, the rival schools might be best summed up as restraint vs. non-restraint. The issue more directly related to the case of the Rev. Mr. Holmes, however, was the fear, much fanned by horror stories gleefully reported in the press – that a family, conniving with sinister madhouse doctors, could manage to lock away sane people for motives almost inevitably financial. *The Medical Times & Gazette*, which decried the cloud under which private asylums such as Heigham Hall were forced to operate, nonetheless summarized the public's concern:

> They are mere mercantile speculations, we are told; the owner
> likes to keep his house full, and therefore is not particular as to the
> state of the wits of those he admits; and whom he once admits
> he is in no hurry to let go free again; indeed, some who come to
> him sane are, by a process of his, rendered in a few weeks perma-
> nently lunatic and therefore his welcome guests for life.

To make the act of committing someone to an asylum more difficult, the Lunatics Act of 1845 required two doctors, duly registered medical practitioners, who are not professionally connected with the institution, to separately examine the patient. They were then required to sign a form stating:

> I, Dr. A, hereby certify that I have this day, separately from any
> other medical practitioner, visited and personally examined Mr. B,
> the person named in the accompanying statement, and that the
> said B is a lunatic and a proper person to be confined, and that I
> formed this opinion from the following fact or facts: *viz*, (Signed)

To falsely sign such a statement was to risk a fine of £20 and the signer would also lay himself open to being sued by the person examined.

With these new precautions in place, the Lunacy Commissioners, as the new overseers of the nation's asylums were to be called, were ever on their guard to protect those who might be wrongfully locked away. Certainly, we can see that the Holmes case was an entirely different affair. In this case, it would be charged that a *sane* person had eagerly claimed to be *insane*, and, in *co-operation with his family*, was locked away rather than face the criminal punishment due him for his heinous crime.

After being approached by the Rev. John Holmes, Dr. Nichols set out promptly to find the required two doctors to certify Edmund's insanity. It was not to be done straightaway. Dr. Frederick Mills of All Saints Green interviewed Edmund and found him to be completely sane. Dr. Robert Hull of Redwell Street declined the commission completely. Finally, two doctors were found to separately interview the clergyman and to put their names to the certificates. They were Dr. William Henry Taylor of Prince's Street in Norwich and Dr. George Gillett, of Brooke. As the resident surgeon in the village controlled by the Holmes family, the pressure placed upon Dr. Gillett to sign seems obvious.

As already stated, the matter of the Rev. Edmund Holmes and his admission to Heigham Hall, however debatably handled, passed quickly from public view. If any thought had been given to questioning the matter, no one had done so for two years. It was not until 1854 that the afore-mentioned Dr. Hull first came forward to make his charge against Dr. W.P. Nichols. Hull claimed that when Nichols came to him asking that he interview the Rev. Holmes, the asylum proprietor had boasted about how he was out to save the clergyman from jail. Nichols went on to say that to get the Rev. Holmes safely inside the asylum would mean "hundreds a year in his pocket." In the first place, Dr. Hull might have seemed a strange choice to do a lunacy interview, as his specialty was the eye, having authored *Cursory Notes on the Morbid Eye*. However, Nichols knew Hull from their work together at the Norfolk & Norwich Hospital. The defenders of Dr. Nichols would ask why, after not having said a thing at the time, Dr. Hull would wait two years to make this accusation, which, if true, would have ruined his erstwhile colleague's reputation.

Word of Dr. Hull's allegation was soon a topic of general discussion. The Norfolk papers demanded an inquiry. It was decided that the case of the Rev. Edmund Holmes would have to be reviewed by the Visiting Justices, a group of local worthies – including Samuel Bignold, the mayor of Norwich, who were charged under the Lunatics Act with visiting all the asylums in their district. They were to inspect the facilities, talk with the patients, and generally ensure the institutions were being properly managed. Recently, the visitors had seen enough to dismiss the medical superintendent of the county pauper's asylum ("reserved for poor lunatics but not for natural born fools or idiots.") There had been no prior issues with the administration of the private asylum at Heigham Hall.

The Visiting Justices met in Norwich in June of 1854. Their first concern was to find out whether the Rev. Holmes had been improperly admitted to Heigham Hall to frustrate the ends of justice. The justices interviewed almost everyone involved in the matter from the time that Mr. Holmes was taken into police hands. Cann, the original magistrate, could not be present but was represented by his son, William Robert Cann, who served as his father's clerk. The younger Cann recalled that his father had quickly concluded that the Rev. Mr. Holmes was mad and he had then decided that the clergyman's friends should be informed that, "if something was done within a certain time, the warrant should not issue to be executed." Young Cann willingly conceded that his father had acted "in consequence of the station of life of Mr. H. Probably, had he been a poor man, the case would have different." Typically, the clerk agreed, that a person would be put on trial first and then make out any plea of lunacy in mitigation.

The elder Cann was not alone in his conclusion that the reverend gentleman was mad. Even the victim's mother, Elizabeth Bunn told the justices that she knew that Mr. H. was "not right in his mind." As a point of interest, Mr. Holmes, during the inquiry, out of deference to his family, was referred to only as "Mr. H." His identity as the Rev. Edmund Holmes was not made public until *The Lancet* published the results of its own investigation in November of 1854. Samuel Barrett, the constable who had taken Mr. H. into custody said he was fully satisfied, good policeman that he was, that the accused was a lunatic. Hannah Bunn, the clergyman's housekeeper, said he was prone to eccentric and even violent behaviour. Her husband, Robert Bunn, said that on one occasion he had had to sit on "Mr. H." for a half-hour, at the least, to prevent him from doing violence to Mrs. Bunn. The Rev. W.W. Andrew, who had known "Mr. H." for so many years, (having called him "neurotic" more than a decade earlier), said that in the weeks just before the assault on the child, the clergyman's conduct had been even more out of the ordinary. He had once told Rev. Andrew that he would likely have to someday kill Mrs. Bunn, the housekeeper, for she was possessed by the soul of seven devils. He never did kill her although one day he tried to choke her by forcing raw potatoes into her mouth. Mr. H. had once told him that the best thing for everyone would be to have him locked away in Norwich Castle.

The visiting justices moved on from the mental state of the Rev. Holmes to the charges against the operators of Heigham Hall. Dr. Robert Hull was, obviously, the star witness for the accusers. The Norwich eye doctor and surgeon swore that Dr. Nichols had come to him to ask that he interview the Rev. Holmes and then sign the certificate of insanity. Hull claimed that Nichols had crowed about plucking the Rev. Holmes away from the law and by being able to admit him to Heigham Hall he stood to earn "hundreds a year" from the grateful Holmes family. Hull stated that he had indignantly refused to participate in the effort and bid Dr. Nichols a good day.

Dr. Nichols appeared next before the visitors and did not deny that he had approached Dr. Hull; he was only one of several physicians he had asked to interview Mr. Holmes. Of course, Nichols emphatically denied making any such boast or like statements as claimed by his former colleague. He said that Dr. Hull had simply declined to see the Rev. Holmes and so he, Dr. Nichols, went elsewhere.

The second issue before the visitors was the discovery that the Rev. Holmes had been so speedily "cured" at Heigham Hall that the doctors were able to discharge their "lunatic" in only two months. The clergyman was then allowed to remain in the asylum as a paying boarder. This was all in clear violation of the Lunacy Acts. Mr. Holmes, with his family still paying his rent regularly, was now serving as chaplain for the male patients. [That other un-named clergyman in residence had presumably not responded as quickly as Mr. Holmes to his regimen of care.] Dr. Nichols insisted that Holmes had undergone a rigorous program of medical and moral treatments and counseling and his "distemper" had been cured. Since assuming the role of chaplain, Mr. Holmes had performed his religious duties with zeal and integrity. There had been no effort to somehow hide the Rev. Mr. Holmes away in the asylum as his presence was duly reported in the quarterly statements prepared for the visiting justices and the Lunacy Commissioners in London. The reports stated that, "Divine service is performed in the house by a clergyman resident in the asylum."

Having heard the evidence, the justices caucused to discuss the matter. Much of the discussion focused on the original action taken by Cann, the magistrate. However mad the Rev. Mr. Holmes may or may not have been, it was wrong to treat a gentleman from a well-known family any differently from anyone else. It would have been much better for everyone had the magistrate allowed the law to take its course and the issue of the accused gentleman's sanity could then be addressed under the established procedures of the criminal courts. In the end, the justices issued the following statement:

> That the Rev. Mr. H. being placed in the asylum, under the circumstances appearing on this enquiry, was rescued from the gripe of the law on a criminal charge.
>
> That the order and medical certificates upon which he was admitted into the asylum were regular, and in the form prescribed in the Act of Parliament in that behalf. In the opinion of the visitors, Mr. H. is not a proper person to have been appointed, or to continue to officiate as, a chaplain to the asylum.
>
> Signed: Mayor Samuel Bignold, J.H. Barnard, Edward Willett, Horatio Bolingbroke, John Sultzer, Samuel S. Beare and C.M. Gibson FRCS.

The Rev. Holmes was then left, once again, an unemployed clergyman, but not for very long. He was soon asked to assist the Rev. William Cobb at his church of St. Margaret's in Norwich. Though he soon settled into his new duties, there would be little peace yet for the Rev. Edmund Holmes. The national press outcry continued. No one cared a whit about whether Mr. Holmes was a fit chaplain for a roomful of lunatics. The great and important issue remained why a man from "an opulent family" had been improperly stashed in a madhouse to escape a criminal trial for the rape of a young girl? On 8 August 1854, the radical member for Marylebone, Lord Dudley Coutts Stewart, put a question to the Home Secretary, Lord Palmerston:

> Lord Dudley Stuart asks the Secretary of State for the Home Department whether he had received a report from the visiting magistrates of the lunatic asylum in Norwich, containing the results of an inquiry by which it appears that justice was evaded on a criminal charge; and whether he would not direct a strict investigation to be made into all the circumstances of the case?

Lord Palmerston thanked "his noble friend" for bringing the matter to his attention and he agreed to forward the question to the Commissioners in Lunacy and he would await their reply.

Timing in life, it is said, is everything. It was then classically bad timing that the license for the proprietors of Heigham Hall to continue the operation of their asylum fell due for renewal by the Norwich city council that October. At the Guildhall, on 24 October 1854, the issue was argued yet again. Nathaniel Palmer, a young barrister from St. Martin's at the Palace and a council member, cited the statements of Dr. Hull, "a man in whom I have the greatest respect" and accused the proprietors of Heigham Hall of "subterfuge" to evade the Lunacy Act regulations. Palmer moved that the license be refused.

Dr. Hull was on hand to once again to recount the day in June of 1852 when Dr. Nichols came to his surgery. His story had now been embellished somewhat. Hull said Nichols told him a clergyman from a high county family had committed a rape and his family "wished to make him out mad." The reverend gentleman himself also wished to be made out mad. Nichols related how he had rescued the man from custody and brought him to Norwich. He needed a second certificate of insanity and once he got it, he defied anyone to remove Mr. Holmes from Heigham Hall. If he got the clergyman admitted, Nichols smiled and added that it would be "hundreds in his pocket." Nichols had even told him how best to interview the Rev. Holmes to get the required conclusion. He was instructed to ask him about how "the devil was inside him prompting him in his actions." Hull told the council that he refused to co-operate and sent Nichols away.

Dr. Nichols was not present at the Quarter Sessions hearing. On hand from the asylum were Dr. John Ferra Watson and the newest partner in the venture, Dr. William Ranking. The latter was a highly respected and frequently published Norfolk physician who had only just been brought in to the partnership by way of re-establishing the facility's credentials. The open talk in Norwich was that Dr. Hull's jealousy of the lofty standing of Dr. Ranking might have been at the root of the whole matter.

Dr. Watson defended the decision to admit the Rev. Mr. Holmes to Heigham Hall. Supporting his statement was a letter received from the Lunacy Commissioners in London:

> Gentlemen, with reference to the correspondence and discussion which has taken place respecting the Rev. H, the Commissioners in Lunacy deem it only fair towards you to say that they are satisfied that when sent to Heigham Hall, he was insane and a proper person to be placed, as such, under medical care in an asylum.
>
> Signed, RWS Lutwidge

Watson next wanted to make clear that, contrary to the wildest stories in the newspapers, Mrs. Bunn's 13-year old daughter had not been raped. "No rape had been perpetrated nor even attempted" by the Rev. Edmund Holmes. An "indecent assault" had been committed, no more. There was never any need to falsify a certificate to have the Rev. Holmes committed. The clergyman's reputation for eccentric and sometimes violent behaviour was well known throughout the neighbourhood. Two years prior to the attack on Mrs. Bunn's daughter, some friends of the Rev. Holmes had enough concern to approach Dr. Nichols to express their worries for the clergyman's mental condition. Dr. Nichols spent a good deal of time observing the Rev. Holmes and talking with him and, at that time, readily decided that there was no need for confinement. After the terrible incident at the Bunn's cottage, however, an overt act had been committed and now the doctors and the Holmes family had to act expeditiously. Once, the Rev. Holmes came to Heigham Hall, he was under Watson's care. The doctor read for the council several entries from his daily logbook. When Holmes first entered the asylum, Watson had noted that the man was very upset and volunteered to give himself up to the police.

When Dr. Watson later invited Holmes to dine with his family – Mrs. Watson, their children and his in-laws all resided with the doctor at the asylum – Holmes declined, saying he was a "morally unsound" man to have around his family. It was a twelve-week effort but Watson said that by September of 1852, the Rev. Mr. Holmes was fully eligible for discharge. Rev. Holmes had asked that he be employed as a chaplain for the other male patients and he had done the work admirably for some eighteen months. So well had he restored his reputation, in fact, that Watson reminded the council that when the visiting justices had directed his removal as "not a proper person," Rev. Holmes had been immediately invited to be a curate at a church in Norwich where he continued to serve without problem.

The final witness to be heard from was Dr. Ranking. He informed the council that he had invested a considerable sum of money in the institution, and stood to lose it all if the license was rejected. He proudly suggested that all the gentlemen present knew well of his reputation and he was quite willing to put that standing in his profession on the line to guarantee the proper operation of Heigham Hall.

The Norfolk Chronicle described the "animated discussion" that followed among the councilmen. John Sultzer, a sewing cotton manufacturer, said that as a visiting justice he had toured Heigham Hall many times.

Never without a feeling of the greatest satisfaction that persons reduced to the deplorable condition of the patients were so well treated with a view to their restitution and recovery. Yet the conduct of one of the proprietors [Nichols] had been as wrong as possible. However, to withhold licensing now would be unfair to the other proprietors. I hope Mr. Palmer will withdraw his opposition but I must repeat that I know of no terms strong enough to express my disapprobation of the conduct of one of the proprietors.

John G. Johnson, a surgeon from St Giles Street, agreed that "a decided irregularity" had been committed. "We deprecate it and we give the proprietors to understand it will not be tolerated in the future." There was much more finger-wagging in the direction of the table where sat two of the three proprietors of Heigham Hall.

The final word, however, would come from Michael Prendergast, QC, Recorder of the City of Norwich. He had chaired the discussion and he closed it by urging that the license be granted. The Recorder declared, "If the license were refused, great loss would fall on the parties interested, and also some public inconvenience would be produced." Presumably, the latter concern had to do with those families who would suddenly be forced to find new homes for the sixty "lunatics" currently housed there. Palmer, bowing to the opinion of the Recorder, said that only because of that honourable gentleman's recommendation would he agree to stand aside and permit the re-licensing of Heigham Hall.

The medical profession, especially those interested in the infant science of psychiatry, had followed the case of the Rev. Holmes with the greatest interest and concern. Dr. Forbes Winslow, who would later be one of the leading "alienists" of his time, said the evidence that the clergyman was truly insane was overwhelming:

In the face of such an amount of testimony, can we draw any other conclusion than that the mind of Mr. Holmes was upset; the contrary would be to suppose that a vast conspiracy existed to establish a fact which no one beyond Mr. Nichols had any interest in making apparent. The fact that the accused have again and again made efforts to be put upon their defense, should have its due consideration; at present they appear ... to have been unfairly assailed, and condemned unheard.

The Lancet, the leading medical journal, also explored the conspiracy issue. While Dr. Nichols was the man who had been singled out for all the obloquy in the matter, he could not have acted alone. He would have needed the co-operation of the magistrates, the police, the two doctors who signed the certificates, the Rev. John Holmes and other members of the deranged cleric's family, and, it must be added, he would also have needed the silence of Dr. Hull – who, if he is to be believed, "for two years harboured a guilty knowledge of a grave offence." As for the original question, was Rev. Holmes sane or insane when admitted to Heigham Hall in June of 1852, *The Lancet* "anxiously" reviewed the evidence and concluded: "The evidence is surely greater in amount and more convincing in character than what has been too often deemed sufficient to make good the allegation of lunacy."

Yet, the question still has to be asked why Dr. Hull had made the claim against Dr. Nichols if it was a falsehood? To be sure, professional jealousy was no more rare in 1852 than it is a century and a half later. *The Lancet* was quite clear on the point, suggesting that raising the issue over two years later "is only to be explained on the supposition that, not from the sense of public duty, but feelings of a personal nature had arisen to instigate proceedings which it was hoped might be prejudicial to the proprietors of the institution."

In a letter to *The Lancet*, accompanying their leading article, Dr. John Ferra Watson suggested that the proprietor's decision to bring into their partnership, Dr. William Ranking, might have been a factor.

> Dr. Hull made the decision two years later to reveal that which had been concealed by him while on friendly terms with Mr. Nichols, and only published when that gentleman united himself with a too successful rival to Dr. Hull in public estimation.

Dr. Hull resigned from the Norfolk & Norwich Hospital that year and he died two years later at the age of 61.

Heigham Hospital, re-licensed, remained in business for another century plus, not closing its doors until 1968. By then, the extensive grounds had been hemmed in by the Norwich sprawl. The scandal of the Holmes case did not long effect the reputation of the asylum. Ten years after all the bad press, in 1864, the institution received a glowing description:

The care that has been taken in securing the most modern sanitary improvements reflects the greatest credit upon the managers, and with all these arrangements there is an artistic decoration which I have rarely seen equaled. The reports of the Commissioners in Lunacy have been unusually favourable to the Institution; and this is not to be wondered at, for all that is said is richly earned.

Dr. WP Nichols remained one of the proprietors into the 1870's.

And, back to the question that serves to title this chapter: was the Rev. Edmund Holmes sane or insane? It seems clear that he was not "right in his mind." He had lived an eccentric life that had prompted comment and concerns long before the incident in 1852. However, and surprisingly, amid all the comment in the medical journals, none of the editorial writers seemed interested in discussing whether a man's lifelong "distemper" – a 53-year old man had indecently assaulted a child of thirteen - could be cured in a matter of only two months? Would anyone today countenance the release of an admitted sex offender after two months? In 1854, however, the Rev. Mr. Holmes was permitted to exit Heigham, having been dispossessed of his role as male chaplain. He went to serve as a curate for the Rev. William Cobb. The vicar of St. Margaret's was also the chaplain at the Norwich jail where he had worked closely with the jail surgeon, Dr. WP Nichols. That might have helped to explain how Mr. Holmes so quickly found employment at St. Margaret's. Regardless, the Rev. Cobb was proud of the "new" Rev. Mr. Holmes:

> During his sojourn in Wymondham, he became less and less responsible for his actions; at the present time, he is as competent to discharge any duty requiring a sound mind as any one; he has, I believe, conducted himself with the strictest propriety during the entire time he has been connected with my parish; he has endeared himself to many of my poor people; and, on all sides, wherever I have heard his name mentioned, it has been with approbation.

Remember, I Am To Have The Housemaid

The Rev. Arthur Loftus, Rector of Fincham.

FINCHAM, IN THE Victorian directories, is uniformly described as a "neat village on the Swaffham road." And so it is today on what is now the A1122. There were once two houses of worship in this well-churched part of England but Fincham St. Michael was pulled down in 1744. Fincham St. Martin remains, a 13th-century structure of flint with a square embattled tower, sitting on a prominence north of the road. For such a small village, the church – with its 83-foot long nave - is quite impressive. An old Fincham rector, Mr. Forby, said but for the "pewing," it would "be the prettiest church in Norfolk."

The Forby family had provided the rectors in Fincham for just over a century, beginning in 1723. In 1825, the Rev. Joseph Forby fainted while taking his bath. The last of the Forby's slipped beneath the soapy waters and drowned. The Forbys and their accomplishments would dominate *The Historical Notices and Records of the Parish of Fincham, County of Norfolk*, as compiled by the Rev. Henry Blyth, who had become rector of the village in 1846.

In obvious embarrassment, however, Mr. Blyth makes only one fleeting mention of the man whom he had succeeded. In the interval of the twenty-one years between the late and lamented Mr. Forby and young Mr. Blyth, the people of Fincham were ministered to by the Rev. Arthur Loftus. Of those two decades, Mr. Blyth – with the greatest possible discretion - dares only to record that the Rev. Mr. Arthur Loftus was "deprived on 12 December 1845."

Few would have predicted that the Rev. Mr. Loftus' career would have ended in such disgrace. His family antecedents were impeccable. His father, the late General William Loftus, had fought at Bunker Hill in the War of the American Revolution, helped crush the Irish rebellion of 1798, and later commanded the garrison at the Tower of London. He sat for many years in Parliament "where he spoke frequently on military matters." Arthur's mother was a daughter of the Marquis of Townshend, a family with great ancestral ties to Norfolk. Arthur, himself, had graduated Cambridge with an M.A.

The Rev. Mr. Loftus was thirty when he arrived in Fincham and took up residence at the old rectory, built in 1624. Rev. Blyth described the building:

> The Rectory House is old, but commodious and well built. It consists of three stories with high pitched roofs and gables…It presents a handsome front to the north, and is well-situated, with its gardens and glebe lands to the south.

Mr. Loftus came to this splendid old rectory unmarried. In fact, he did not marry until the age of forty when he wed Mary Ann Ray Clayton. She was thirty and the only child of a nearby clergyman; her father, the Rev. William Ray Clayton was the rector of Great and Little Ryburgh, small villages near Fakenham. Alas, Arthur and Mary Ann were ill-suited to one another and the marriage was never a happy one. They managed to have three children but each confinement had been very difficult for Mary Ann. The children were all born prematurely, only two of them surviving. Mary Ann's mother – who was frequently at the rectory and especially during her daughter's pregnancies – put the blame for these difficulties on Arthur's violent temper and abuse. Days after the second child's birth, with Mary Ann still quite weak, Mrs. Clayton claimed that Arthur put himself into such a fit of passion that he terrified them all, especially Mary Ann, giving rise to fears that her "intellects would be affected." For his part, Arthur had become convinced that he had married well below his station. He regularly insulted his mother-in-law and, while on holiday in Cromer, he told Mary Ann that any one of her housemaids had come from a better family. In early 1840, Mary Ann (and her mother) left Fincham and returned to her father's rectory. Arthur made several unsuccessful efforts to retrieve his wife. His cousin, Lord James Townshend, acted as mediator but without any more satisfaction. In 1841, by the laws of the day, the Rev. Loftus was forced to go to court to file a suit for restoration of his conjugal rights.

The case was heard before an Ecclesiastical Court at the Cathedral in Norwich, the "worshipful" Charles Evans, Chancellor of the Diocese of Norwich, presiding. The publicity generated "from the known respectability of the parties" had served to "excite great interest." The counsel for Mrs. Loftus told the court that the Rev. Mr. Loftus had been consistently abusive to his wife, both verbally and physically. The abuse led her to have several miscarriages and both of their surviving children had been born prematurely. Several servants were called to support the claim but it was later shown that most of them had been sacked by the rector and since hired by Mrs. Loftus or her mother. This, to be certain, weakened their credibility. As for Mrs. Clayton, the presiding official concluded that she "appeared to entertain a prejudice against her son-in-law." The Rev. Mr. Loftus, in his turn, presented a series of character witnesses, eighteen (!) in number, clergy and lay, many from Fincham, who all made the case that the rector had been "uniformly kind" to his wife. Several witnesses, in fact, swore that Mrs. Loftus had personally remarked to them about how well she had been treated by her husband.

In the end, Chancellor Evans ruled that there was no evidence to support the claim of cruelty and abuse. While the language used by the rector of Fincham towards his wife and her mother was deplorable "whatever the irritation he had received," there was no proof of actual physical violence. The claim that Mrs. Loftus' confinements had been affected by her husband's behaviour came solely from Mrs. Clayton and had not been supported by any medical witnesses.

The testimony of the ex-Loftus servants now employed by the Claytons was described as "very suspicious." What seemed to have happened, surmised Mr. Evans, was a falling out caused by the (not all that unusual) interference of the bride's mother. Additionally, there were difficulties with the servants. Neither of these issues would establish a legal reason for any wife to abandon her rightful place by her husband.

He concluded by citing the opinion of Sir William Scott in the [then] ruling case of *Evans v Evans*:

> What merely wounds the mental feelings ... petulance ... rudeness ... even occasional sallies of temper, if they do not threaten bodily harm, do not amount to legal cruelty; they are high moral offences in the marriage state undoubtedly, not innocent surely in any state of life, but still they are not that cruelty against which the law can relieve.

Therefore, Mr. Loftus was fully entitled to the judgment and Mary Ann was "duly admonished" to return to her husband.

Rev. Loftus might well have had his legal victory but there was no happily ever after. He would not have his wife. She remained with her family. In the previous century, he might well have abducted her and had her locked in the rectory. In the enlightened climate of early Victorian England, however, such a stratagem was not the thing. Not to say it wasn't done: in 1856, a Berkshire clergyman (Rev. Henry Cherry of Burghfield) did just that and was forced by public outrage to release the imprisoned Mrs. Cherry within hours. Mary Ann Loftus' refusal to obey the court did give her husband legal standing to withhold or reduce his financial support. However, as for his "conjugal rights" as we know them, he was going to have to do without. What was a man to do? This loss of consortium soon appeared to be having a significantly deleterious impact on the rector's health. He brought his cares and needs to his Fincham physician, Dr. Edward Arthy. The helpful medico made the suggestion that perhaps Mr. Loftus might want to find a woman, a mistress, somewhere some distance away. With discretion it could be done and, if the clergyman "got in a little scrape," the good surgeon would be ready to explain his behaviour. Readers should know well in advance that Dr. Arthy would later insist his advice was given with a wink and was meant to be taken as a bit of a jest. If so, the joke part failed to register with Mr. Loftus.

The rector, taking his doctor's counsel to heart, began to regularly frequent a brothel in King's Lynn. In his defense, he was hardly alone. A contemporary health official remarked upon King's Lynn reputation for debauchery, "Prostitution is carried on to a greater extent than any town I have lived in." Out of all of the "houses of ill-fame" from which to choose in Lynn, the rector selected one in Birdcage Row under the management of a woman by the name of "Mrs." Sconce.

Loftus was happy to be accompanied on these romps by his faithful manservant, Henry Twiddy. His consortium renewed, the Rev. Loftus' spirits rallied. He was, nonetheless, troubled. Through no fault of Mrs. Sconce or her willing and desirable ladies – King's Lynn was but a mere dozen miles from Fincham. This proximity to his parish most likely did not meet the Arthy test for "some distance away." There would always be the risk of encountering some nosy villagers who might wonder why their clergyman was to be seen toddling about in such dodgy purlieus as Birdcage Row. The Rev. Loftus, sensibly it must be conceded, inquired of the Sconce woman if she was aware of another such venue just that bit farther away. Of course, she was.

Soon, the rector and Twiddy had taken their passions around The Wash to Boston in Lincolnshire. There, in the phallic shadow of the famous Boston Stump, Mr. Loftus would now bring his custom. The number of brothels in Boston had doubled in the early Victorian years; the Mayor went so far as to decry that "it was frequently remarked to him by strangers, that Boston, in the number and boldness of its prostitutes, bore a terrible pre-eminence over any town in the kingdom." Mr. Loftus and Twiddy found themselves soon doing business with a "Mrs. Mary Foreman." The clergyman and his faithful Twiddy were soon delighted with the allurements of the ladies in Mrs. Foreman's employ. It was, however, a roundtrip of nearly one hundred miles between Fincham and Boston. While Mr. Loftus would leave a curate behind at the rectory, it was unwise and would surely lead to comment if he were unexplainably away too often. A plan was therefore hatched. The rector approached Mrs. Foreman with an offer to hire two of his favourite courtesans to return with him to Fincham. Mrs. Foreman had her price and a deal was struck. Jemima Cross and Sarah (sometimes called Susan) Warsop agreed - if they had any choice in the matter at all - to take leave of their old (oldest?) profession and be carted off with Mr. Loftus and Twiddy to begin new lives as rectory servants in Fincham. Jemima was now to be the housemaid and Sarah would handle the cooking. Jemima would later recall the day they all crossed the threshold of the rectory and hearing Mr. Loftus flatly tell Twiddy, "Remember, Henry, I am to have the housemaid and you shall have the cook." Welcome, ladies, to Fincham rectory!

This happy division of labour and pleasure continued for some weeks. Eventually, the gentlemen must have tired of their assigned concubine and, for variety sake, if naught else, they opted to exchange mistresses. Soon, all but the rector had come down with venereal disease. Worse news yet followed when Jemima reported that she was pregnant. That unforeseen difficulty was overcome by resorting to a traditional *emmenagogue:* a concoction of dried and crushed bay leaves and berries, which Jemima then washed down with a beaker of gin. It had the desired effect. Nevertheless, it was a close call and set the Rev. Mr. Loftus to considering what would be best for his menagerie. Jemima, it seems, was not working out. It would be best to send her away. Being a kindly sort of man, however, Mr. Loftus found her another position in service (a safe distance away) and even wrote a most glowing reference for his erstwhile lover. Jemima, of course, would have to be replaced. Someone must be found to assume her duties of both making and occupying the rector's bed. Mrs. Foreman's "agency" was once again employed and a young lady of serviceable talents named Maria Ward had soon come thither and restored the sexual harmonies of Fincham Rectory.

Such a highly irregular domestic establishment in the home of a clergyman could not go unnoticed in a village the size of Fincham. So offensive was all of this misconduct that Mr. Loftus's aforementioned curate – the Rev. F.J. Ball – gave notice and took his leave from Fincham altogether. The tipping point, however, came with Jemima's sudden departure, amid the village gossip of her pregnancy. Word of these suspicions and rumours had reached the friends of Mrs. Loftus' interests who demanded that the Bishop of Norwich begin an investigation. A preliminary inquiry, conducted by a panel of local clergyman, found enough *prima facie* evidence to send the matter to the Court of Arches in London. The rector of Fincham was being formally accused of adultery and incontinence, specifically: "frequenting houses of ill-fame, having intercourse with prostitutes, hiring women of that description as servants, and having carnal intercourse with them."

The Court of Arches takes its name from the days when the ecclesiastical court convened in the crypt of the church of St. Mary le Bow or St. Mary of the Arches. By 1845, the court had long been in place in Doctor's Commons, in St. Paul Churchyard. The Dean of Arches was Dr. Herbert Jenner Fust.

> In old Sir Herbert's later days it was no mere pleasantry, or bold figure of speech, to say that the court had risen, for he used to be lifted from his chair and carried bodily from the chamber of justice by two brawny footmen. Of course, as soon as the judge was about to be elevated by his bearers, the bar

rose; and, also as a matter of course, the bar continued to stand until the strong porters had conveyed their weighty and venerable burden along the platform behind one of the rows of advocates and out of sight.

In the case of the Rev. Mr. Loftus, Fust ruled that, owing to the "exceedingly grave" nature of the charges, all testimony would be taken behind closed doors. This was a great and understandable disappointment to the press and public. However, from Mr. Fust's verdict, issued in December 1845, it is clear that the leading witness against the rector was Jemima Scott. As already seen, when she had been first brought to Fincham, the rector had staked his claim to her as his favourite. Soon, however, he had exchanged her for Sarah and then, when Jemima became pregnant, he sent her packing altogether. Jemima was not a woman to take well to such a speedy fall from clerical favour. She said her pregnancy had ended in early March of 1844; she stated that Sarah had given her the potion that caused either a miscarriage or an abortion. The rector had then sent her away but with a letter stating: "Jemima Scott is honest and understands the duties of a housemaid; she left from the situation being too much for her strength." Fust conceded that Jemima was a witness of a very low character who, by her lights, clearly held a serious grudge against the accused. This would make her evidence – if unsupported – very suspect indeed.

However, Jemima's recollection of life at the rectory was, to a great degree, reinforced by the testimony of Sarah Warsop – or Sarah Barkham, to give the young lady her due, as she had taken (perhaps) the first step to reform by recently contracting a marriage of her own. She admitted having been employed by Mrs. Foreman, a woman she described ecumenically as a "good Methodist." Sarah, as Mr. Fust noted, was a reluctant witness; he thought that made her evidence all the more valuable, since the ex-rectory cook seemed "to be activated by feelings favourable" to the Rev. Loftus. Importantly, however, Sarah had confirmed the nature of the arrangements at the rectory and also described how she had prepared the bayleaf nostrum for Jemima. She insisted that the rector, although he was certainly aware of Jemima's condition, had not participated in these abortifacient preparations. Sarah also said that both she and Jemima were certain that Twiddy was the man responsible for the venereal disease outbreak at Fincham rectory. Lastly, the witness threw a bit of help the rector's way, by testifying that her "co-worker" Jemima was a very bitter and profligate woman who would say anything to get revenge against anyone who had wronged her.

Dr. Frederick Gent, the second doctor in Fincham, testified that he had treated three of the rectory denizens for "cupid's itch." According to a report in *The Lancet* of 1841, "There are few points of surgical practice that have undergone a more complete revolution within the past few years than has the method of treatment of the venereal disease." Mercury, long relied on by doctors, was under attack for being as "productive of effects as injurious as the disease." Mercurialists warred with non-mercurialists.

An ecclesiastical court was certainly no place for that argument to continue. Dr. Gent therefore did not reveal to the court his own treatment protocols; however, and more importantly, he did insist that the Rev. Loftus had not required any ministrations for such an affliction.

Both brothel keepers testified to Mr. Loftus' regular patronage. Hannah Payne, one of Mrs. Sconces' trollops in King's Lynn, said she had personally seen the Rev. Loftus at her establishment on four occasions and she had slept with him twice. She recalled that the clergyman had told her that he was a married man living apart from his wife and his doctor had ordered him to "have women." Mrs. Sconce, unhappily "confined to her bed owing to poor health," was not able to attend the proceedings. Mrs. Foreman came down from Boston to contribute the curious details of her arrangement to part with her young ladies who would be taken in to the rector's "service." Interestingly, Mr. Twiddy, whose testimony would have presumably been vital to either side, does not appear to have had any role in the inquiry – other, of course, than as a lusty participant in the salacious conduct alleged.

The Rev. Mr. Loftus had chosen his counsel well. Herbert Jenner was the son (albeit one of fourteen children) of the Dean of Arches, Dr. Jenner Fust. The son would argue the defense case before the father. The younger Jenner acknowledged the weight of the sensational evidence already heard. However, can the court put any faith in the testimony taken from such slatterns and their procuresses? Offsetting such loathsome persons, the defense would again parade the surprisingly loyal cadre of character witnesses for Mr. Loftus: Sir Thomas Hare of Stow Hall, the largest landowner in the area; and representative local clergy, including the Rev. George Henry Dashwood of Stow Bardolph and the Rev. W.G. Townley, one of the rural deans in the diocese of Norwich. These witnesses, and more, entered the box to suggest that the allegations were totally out of character with the good and decent country clergyman they all knew. The Rev. Loftus of their acquaintance was a man "remarkably guarded in his conduct and language and a man of refinement and high breeding." They "never had a suspicion or surmise" of the salacious goings on at the rectory in Fincham. Significantly, and it was not lost upon the Dean of Arches, Mr. Ball, the wretched curate, was not on the list of character witnesses.

Dr. Arthy was called to explain the nature of his rather unique prescription for the rector's condition. The physician said that it must be remembered that Mrs. Loftus had left her husband three years before and she had refused to obey a court order to return to her bed and board. The Rev. Mr. Loftus was thereby left in a "highly excited state." He and the rector had a conversation in which he suggested that Mr. Loftus might, as many an English gentleman in a like predicament had done, discreetly "cohabit occasionally with a decent female" somewhere away from Fincham. This idea of prescribing "fornication" was not at all unusual at the time:

> The question of morality did not belong to the physician; but *a man must not expect to be in health, if he neglected to exercise a natural function.*

The great Victorian physician Sir James Paget, however, thoroughly opposed the idea of prescribing harlotry:

> I would just as soon prescribe theft or lying, or anything else that God has forbidden. If men will practice fornication or uncleanness, it must be of their own choice and their sole responsibility … Chastity does no harm to mind or body; its discipline is excellent; marriage can be waited for. Among the many nervous and hypochondriacal patients who have talked to me about fornication, I have never heard one say he was better or happier after it; several have said they were worse; and many, having failed, have been made much worse.

In Fincham, far removed from such debates going on in the surgeries of Harley Street, Dr. Arthy and his rector had their little discussion on the matter. The doctor suggested that if the rector's "cohabitation" somehow became known, and there was a "scrape" over it, then the physician vowed he would do what he could to explain the situation. Dr. Arthy, however, insisted to Dr. Fust that he had made the suggestion more in jest than as a prescription. Moreover, he did not think that the rector's conduct, if proven true, had followed the letter of his advice since he had advised that Mr. Loftus should restrict any such romantic escapades to "decent" females. The clergyman had unfortunately opted for the fruit closer to the ground.

In his closing statement, the younger Jenner said that the testimony of these tawdry witnesses for the prosecution was contradictory, inconsistent and – as the character witnesses have stated – highly improbable. If these witnesses are to be believed, then no man is safe from having his name slandered. Any man could have walked into Mrs. Sconce's brothel and declared himself to be the Rev. Arthur Loftus. Nor could one single resident of Fincham be found to testify to any public scandal. This entire sordid series of events was likely set in motion by the indiscreet suggestions of Dr. Arthy, whom Jenner described as a "good natured but overly talkative" fellow. Arthy's ribald advice, ill-advisedly repeated in the village, began a series of rumours that were greedily seized upon by Mrs. Loftus and her vengeful family. It was their inveterate loathing of Mr. Loftus that had led them to conspire with this assortment of despicable characters to defame this clergyman and bid to ruin his life and career.

Having taken his customary time to deliberate the fate of Mr. Loftus, Fust issued his ruling on 12 December 1845. He conceded that it was highly improbable that a clergyman could be thought to have abandoned himself to such a degree of depravity as was here charged. To believe it was to credit the testimony of prostitutes and brothel-keepers. Still, there it was. Sarah supported Jemima. Witnesses placed Mr. Loftus and Twiddy at both brothels. There was evidence that the two women and Twiddy had been treated for venereal disease. While some might suggest that this goes to show that the rector was not involved in their carnality, it does not excuse him for allowing such conduct within his own household. In his favour, there was no proof that Mr. Loftus was party to the termination of Jemima's pregnancy. He was, however, fully knowledgeable of her profession and her condition and yet he wrote a reference for her next employer. This was hardly proper conduct for a man of the church. Twiddy's behaviour as guide and procurer throughout was disgusting. Imagine how degrading it must be for a clergyman, not only to merely have such a man in his household, but to be seen associating with him in houses of prostitution. Let no one attempt to excuse Mr. Loftus or suggest he was misled or gulled into bringing these women into his home. "Unless Mr. Loftus is a perfect idiot, he could not suffer himself to be so blinded as to the character of these persons." The testimony of so many clergymen to Mr. Loftus' good character could not overcome the telling decision by the accused not to call as a supporting witness the Rev. Mr. Ball, the one clergyman who had lived in the closest proximity to him. The defense had argued that it was improbable that a respected clergyman would have done any of this. Individually, the actions might have seemed improbable. When all of the evidence was considered, however, Dr. Fust said the improbability vanished. Therefore, the charges having been fully and substantially proven, Mr. Loftus was found guilty of engaging in the most profligate conduct. There was nothing to do but impose the then ultimate punishment:

> Herbert Jenner Fust, Knight, Doctor of Laws, having first called upon the name of Christ, and setting God alone before our eyes, having maturely deliberated upon the proceedings had in the said cause, and in the offences proved exacting by law deprivation of ecclesiastical promotion, have thought fit to pronounce, and do accordingly hereby pronounce, decree and declare that the said Rev. Arthur Loftus, Clerk, by reason of the premises, ought by law to be deprived of all his ecclesiastical promotions within the said province of Canterbury, and especially of the said united vicarage of Fincham St. Martin and rectory of Fincham St. Michael …

His professional fall and disgrace was complete; Loftus was also, apparently abandoned by his family. In the 1847 edition of *Burke's Genealogical and Heraldic Dictionary of the Landed Gentry of Great Britain and Ireland*, the Rev. Loftus's name is completely omitted from the family lineage. He did live another forty years, surviving his poor wife who died in 1856. Identified in the census as a widower and "the former rector of Fincham," Loftus spent the last years of his life living (and moving about) with a mysterious "South American merchant," Emmanuel Paminara. Interestingly, Paminara was registered as having been born in King's Lynn! The two moved from Islington to Southend to Penge where they were joined in South London by two of Paminara's "nieces" from British Columbia. Loftus died in 1884 at the age of 88

I Will Beat You No Longer

The Rev. Bryan O'Malley, Vicar of Flitcham

It is a funny way to save souls to give money for having no souls to cure in rich sinecures, and to leave even many souls upon very little money, or upon what their vicars can pick up. *The Plundered Church* (1880) by the Rev. Bryan O'Malley, vicar of St. Mary's, Flitcham, Norfolk.

THE INEQUALITY of the distribution of the great wealth of the Church of England was a commonplace subject for debate and argument in late Victorian England. One of the most quarrelsome participants in this discussion was the Irish born parson, the Rev. Mr. Bryan O'Malley.

In 1873, he had come to be vicar of the small village of Flitcham in West Norfolk. Though Flitcham was a well-situated place - "lying in a picturesque valley" – it was otherwise a poor and neglected parish. O'Malley came to the crumbling church of St. Mary the Virgin. When he arrived, what did he find but the chancel gone, the south transept dilapidated, and the roof in full need of repair. And he without the means to do anything about it. What most sorely provoked O'Malley, however, was that, only a mile or so across the fields, stood the splendid church of St. Mary Magdalene. The map shows that Flitcham lies on the edge of the Sandringham estate, the then relatively new country seat of the Prince of Wales. Though

Sandringham parish had not one quarter of the 400 "souls" that lived in Flitcham, the church there had a, well, princely endowment. Yet, so near, the poor of Flitcham were supposed to worship in a leaking church, with animals grazing in and soiling the churchyard. They were consigned to hear God's word from a vicar clad in a hand-me-down frayed surplice. While at Sandringham, the rector in his splendid vestments preached amidst "richly stained" glass, royal memorials and a new organ donated by HRH the Prince of Wales. And what was God's reward for bestowing such luxury, O'Malley asked? Sandringham church was half full at best with only the most desultory worshippers. Few of Prince "Bertie's" set, who had made Sandringham, in effect, Marlborough House north, could even manage to rouse themselves for worship after their "balls and dances, sporting and general frolicking and affected grandeur."

The Rev. Bryan O'Malley was not a man to suffer all this in silence. He raised a ruckus about the unfairness of the distribution of the Church's great wealth. He badgered the Bishop of Norwich. He was not ashamed to admit to begging from the great local landowner, the Earl of Leicester. Rev. O'Malley, through most of the late 1870's, walked hundreds of miles, across Norfolk and beyond, into Suffolk, into the Fens, seeking contributions. After a while, he could see people closing their doors or running the other way, knowing what they were thinking, "Here comes that wild Irish parson with his shillelagh." Notwithstanding the frequent rebuffs, it was a successful campaign; Lord Leicester footed the bill for restoring St. Mary's – a new roof, a new vestry and (for the sensitivities of the Flitcham worshippers) his Lordship deigned to restrain his tenants from any longer grazing their livestock in the glebe. O'Malley's footsore efforts raised an additional £2000 with which to endow the church and raise the vicar's annual pay from a meager £80 to £200. Never a shy man, in 1880, O'Malley wrote a several hundred page triumphant screed entitled *The Plundered Church,* and gave himself the bulk of the credit:

> [I have] removed the curtain which conceals the crafty proceedings of those worldly Bishops, and of those aspiring Church dignitaries, who act as if they kept poor vicars starved and degraded on purpose, to secure homage to themselves and to enable them to appear the greater and grander by the contrast.

Understandably, praise poured in for the doughty Rev. Bryan O'Malley. In *White's Directory for Norfolk,* contemporary readers were informed that

Flitcham parish church had been restored, in great part, "by the exertions of the present incumbent who literally tramped the country for the purpose." It is therefore with reluctance that it must be reported that simultaneously with his passionate and embittered fund-raising drive, the Rev. Bryan O'Malley was enmeshed in an equally, if not more so, passionate and embittered marriage. The case of *O'Malley v O'Malley* made sensational headlines in the very same year that the restored Flitcham church re-opened.

The Rev. Bryan O'Malley had crossed the Irish Sea with an M.A. from Trinity College, Dublin. He began his church career as a curate in Norfolk, including a stay in the village of Congham. His prospects for advancement in the church were undoubtedly much improved when, in March of 1872, he married Frances Keppel. She was the sixth of thirteen children born to another Norfolk clergyman. The Keppels, however, were an historic Norfolk family of great achievements – in the church, the navy and in the peerage. After her father's early death, Frances' interests had been looked after by her uncle, the 6th Earl of Albemarle. The Keppels surely must have viewed with some wonderment Frances' decision - at the then rather late age of 34 – to marry a curate. Nonetheless, the family blessed the union by pulling the requisite strings to get the young groom his first parish – albeit in impoverished Flitcham. First, however, after their wedding at Little Walsingham church, the O'Malleys would take a honeymoon in Ireland.

Frances would later claim that, within a fortnight of their marriage, while in Ireland, her husband struck her with a stick. There were fierce arguments. She threatened to leave him straightaway and return to England. Bryan expressed his repentance and vowed to mend his ways. This pattern would be repeated many more times. In Flitcham, children came in rather rapid succession, four in five years, three sons and a daughter. This rapid growth of the O'Malley clan much troubled the vicar as the extra costs put pressure on the already limited income of his church. O'Malley turned to his Saviour: "I prayed to God to give me no more children as they were disendowing me as causing expenses for doctors, monthly nurses (etc)." There were no more O'Malley children. Perhaps, however, that was less due to prayer than to the fact that Mrs. O'Malley had finally left her husband after another of his violent attacks.

Money was a frequent spark to their quarrels. It must have been a shock to Frances, who had grown up knowing only her father's lavishly furnished church fitted out with the Keppel fortune. St. Mary's, North

Creake, was renowned for its size and the magnificent nave overlooked by angels carved in an ornate 15th century roof. Now, she had come to a village church that hardly had a roof at all, more of a crumbling pile in grounds more resembling a barnyard than a place of worship. While Bryan traipsed the countryside with his shillelagh, Frances and the children scraped by at Flitcham vicarage, relying increasingly on handouts from the Keppel relations. This provoked more arguments as Bryan claimed that his wife openly mocked his "low born" Irish roots. Adding more peat to this fire was the presence of O'Malley's 83-year old widowed mother, Honora, who spoke no English. It's also worthwhile noting that the first of the children to arrive was named Bryan, for his father. Then came another son, Lewis, and the daughter, Grace. The final boy, however, got the full Keppel treatment, Albemarle Barrett-Lennard O'Malley!

The disputes between the O'Malleys invariably ended with something, whatever was to hand, being thrown at one another. Manure (the churchyard was a ready source), coins, knives, boiling water; Frances would even swear that Bryan frequently hurled his Bible at her. And there were more beatings. Frances said he struck her with an umbrella, a rope, several sticks and, once again, the Bible, always nearby at the vicarage.

In 1880, Frances had determined that, for her safety and sanity, she would leave her husband and take the children with her. One of her brothers – yet another Keppel clergyman – the Rev. George Keppel came with his carriage to remove his sister and the little ones from Flitcham. While the Rev. Keppel was handing the children in one door of the carriage, the Rev. O'Malley was taking them out the opposite door and ordering the youngsters back into the vicarage. O'Malley again pleaded with the Keppel forces arrayed against him for that proverbial last chance. In front of his brother-in-law, O'Malley promised Frances – "I will beat you no more." Given the vicar's depressing habit of going back on such promises repeatedly, it was thought advisable to put this pledge down in writing.

In a statement dated 14 August 1880, the Rev. O'Malley pledged:

> In consideration that my wife will return to cohabitation with me, I hereby promise and undertake that in the future I will not be guilty of any acts of violence or ill conduct towards her by word or deed. And, further, in case I shall fail in performance of this promise, such return to cohabitation shall not be considered or taken advantage of as condonation of past occurrences or differences. Signed, the Rev. Bryan O'Malley

Dated the same day, Frances wrote her response:

> In consideration of the above promise on the other side, I hereby promise to return to cohabitation with my husband, and to be to him a faithful and dutiful wife. Signed, Frances O'Malley

The combat between the O'Malleys was, of course, not unnoticed in the village. Many of the more violent scenes were enacted in front of the servants. Word of such "evil reports" would inevitably reach the Bishop in Norwich and preliminary inquiries were set afoot into the suitability of this troublesome vicar of Flitcham. On 2 September 1880, Frances agreed – in the new spirit of co-operation that had been established – to write to the Bishop regarding "certain reports which are calculated to damage my husband and the cause of religion." She stated:

> It is not true that my husband has ever treated me with any violence, or that he has ever done me any bodily injury. It is not true that he has ever struck me with a stick, or any weapon, or with his fist. Neither is it true that he has struck me with a knife, or touched me with it, or that he has thrown it at my person. It is not true that he has turned me and my sister out of doors or that he tore my clothes in May as reported. Neither is it true that he starved me without giving me enough food. It is untrue that he shut me up all night in our kitchen, naked, without food or clothing of any sort. He has never shut me up at all. There is no truth whatever in saying that some dirty indescribable thing was done or found in the vessels we have for kitchen use.

The mind (and stomach?) cannot but reel at the possibilities suggested by the last of the poor woman's denials. Mrs. O'Malley informed the Bishop that the source of this extraordinary list of calumnies was either unhappy local tradesmen who wanted their bills paid or wealthy local clergy who had felt the wrath of the Rev. O'Malley's comments on their "affected grandeur." The O'Malley inquiry was allowed to close.

This *entente cordiale* at Flitcham vicarage was, predictably, not to be a long lasting one. In November, following an argument, O'Malley locked his wife and their daughter out of the house. Frances had to appeal to the laundress who had arrived for her chores to let her in through the servant's entrance. This was surely demeaning to a vicar's wife, let alone a Keppel and the niece of an Earl. Then, the following day, 21 November 1880, after a night's snowfall, O'Malley ordered his wife and children to leave the vicarage.

Winter had come early to north Norfolk in 1880. Across the snow covered fields in Sandringham, the Prince of Wales was entertaining Prime Minister Gladstone. According to *The Penny Illustrated Paper*, the Prince had "expressed himself anxious about the health of the Premier, and, with a view to the inclemency of the weather, pressed upon him the loan of a fur coat, which W.E.G. gratefully but firmly declined." No such solicitousness was to be shown by the rector of Flitcham. The five O'Malleys – without a proffered fur wrap between them – had to trudge through the snow to the nearest church. At Hillington rectory, the Rev. Henry Ffolkes admitted the chilled refugees and remembered that on that cold November day, the children were without any hats or scarves.

Frances O'Malley and her children would not return to Flitcham. They took lodgings in Richmond Road, London and Mrs. O'Malley employed the leading divorce counsel of the day to handle her request for a judicial separation on grounds of cruelty. She would also seek custody of the children.

Frederick Inderwick QC began the proceedings on 23 July 1881 by describing the O'Malleys marriage as a "story of continual ill-treatment with periods of happiness." Frances took the stand to relate that while on her honeymoon, she was struck by her husband for the first time. She ran through an eight-year litany of assaults. He grabbed her by the hair and pulled out enough of it to leave a bald spot. He hit her with umbrellas and sticks and – as we know – the good book itself. He threw a knife at her that missed and struck a servant in the hand. He poured boiling water in her lap. He called her names so vile that she begged the presiding judge, Sir James Hannen, not to force her to use them in court. Her husband demeaned her in front of the servants and the village by forcing her to hoe potatoes in the garden. He made her clean the barnyard detritus from his boots and would throw them back at her if she hadn't done a satisfactory job.

Frances then described the series of events in the summer and fall of 1880 that prompted her to make a final break from Flitcham. Her family had long urged her to leave the vicarage but she gave her husband a last chance. In her brother's presence, Bryan had promised "I will beat you no longer." He also made his written pledge that he would "not be guilty of any violence or ill-conduct towards her." She also pledged, in return, to "be to him a faithful and dutiful wife." She freely admitted writing the letter of 2 September 1880 to the Bishop of Norwich in which she flatly denied that her husband had ever been violent to her. She testified, however, that she had been cowed into writing that letter and her husband stood over her as she wrote it. After a final confrontation in November, her husband ordered her to leave the vicarage and – without allowing her to properly dress herself or the children – they were all locked out and forced to walk to Hillington in two inches of new fallen snow.

Richard Searle was the counsel for the Rev. Bryan O'Malley. He rose to ask Frances about her feelings for her husband. She was from a very wealthy and respected family, with close relations in the peerage and in more fashionable clerical circumstances and yet she married this poor Irish parson. She said that when she married him it was a "love match." Even Sir James enjoyed a chuckle on the bench over that as laughter erupted in the courtroom. Searle suggested that no one could blame her for being bitter and argumentative when someone of her upbringing found herself in this grim and impecunious parish of Flitcham. But she denied picking fights or constantly complaining about money. She swore that she had never told anyone that she had always regretted she married an O'Malley because they were "low born" people.

As for the violence at Flitcham vicarage, Frances insisted that she did not give as good as she got. She denied ever throwing a fireplace poker at her husband. She would - when angry - throw things back at him but she never began the hostilities. She admitted throwing a penny in his face when he had given one to her for cleaning his boots. She threw it back in disgust. She conceded that she had written the exculpatory letter to the Bishop on her husband's behalf but again swore that it had been dictated to her and written under duress. Searle could only ask, why, then, she had permitted herself to remain in the vicarage for another two months?

Several witnesses were called to support Frances' description of her life with the vicar of Flitcham. Her brother, the Rev. George Keppel, testified to his being at the vicarage on the day of the carriage incident. He heard Bryan tell Frances, "I will beat you no longer."

Mrs. Trundle, the vicarage housekeeper, was the poor woman struck with the errant flying knife the vicar had hurled at his wife. Mrs. Trundle said it struck her hand and left a nasty cut. She also testified to having witnessed several similar arguments with the inevitable ensuing flying debris. Mrs. Trundle said her heart had always gone out to Frances as she thought the vicar's wife was always "very loving" to her husband. Another occasional servant, Laura Skate, recalled that she heard the vicar tell the children their mother was a "devil" and they should "go and kick the brute."

Finally, the Rev. Henry Edward Ffolkes recalled the day in the previous November when Mrs. O'Malley and her four children arrived at Hillington rectory. It was a bitter day, after an unseasonably early snow. The children were all quite chilled having made the walk without any hats or scarves. The evidence of the hatless bairns was important not only out of a mother's worry that they might catch a cold; it also established the Rev. O'Malley's cruelty to his own children by sending them out unprepared for the weather, an important issue for the question of custody. Rev. Ffolkes testified that he and his wife made every effort to warm and feed the O'Malleys in their distress. Hillington rectory, depending upon the path taken, was perhaps a mile and a half from Flitcham.

The defense of the Rev. Bryan O'Malley would be left entirely up to him. There were tellingly none of the customary character witnesses willing to come forward to testify to his true loving nature or what a good father he was to his children. The vicar's only loyal witness was his mother but she was in her eighties and spoke no English. Somehow she managed to make it clear that – in her mind anyway – her son had always been kind to his wife; he had never slapped Frances or hit her with a stick. Alas, since no one in court knew the Gaeltacht, Honora O'Malley's presence as a witness – to quote one of the press accounts – was worthless. It would be all on the vicar of Flitcham.

O'Malley could not deny that he was a passionate man, quick to anger. He had written in *The Plundered Church* about his "hot Irish blood," and his "natural Irish course of using a vocal trumpet." He, however, insisted he was not a violent man and certainly never one to his wife. Whilst his counsel, Mr. Searle, read through Mrs. O'Malley's charges against him, the vicar replied to each, in a firm Irish voice, "Nothing of the sort ever happened," or "No foundation whatever." Occasionally, he would offer an explanation. As for the boiling water that spilled on Mrs. O'Malley, he and his wife had been struggling to get their youngest to take his bath and the water basin had been overturned by accident.

O'Malley said his wife was an extremely difficult woman who resented bitterly her husband's standing as a poor clergyman. Frances was a Keppel. He was nothing. He was earning just £80 a year until by his own efforts, begging and walking hundreds of miles, he raised the endowment to bring himself and future vicars a comfortable living. (Interestingly, Rev. George Keppel had contributed £50.) Still, she resented doing the chores that face the wives of all poor country clergymen. She didn't like working in the vegetable garden as it was beneath her. She had no objection, though, to tend her own flowerbeds. They cleaned each other's boots, as all countryside couples must do.

Once, by way of thanks, he gave her a penny and tried to kiss her, she threw the coin at him and struck him in the eye. A painful welt was with him for some time.

While not denying that their arguments were frequently heated, O'Malley again swore that there was never any physical violence. He insisted that Frances did not write the 2 September letter to the Bishop of Norwich under any duress. It was, rather, a truthful statement, voluntarily given by her, placing the blame for the lies told against him where it belongs – with grasping Norfolk tradesmen and snobbish local clergymen, men he had called "rich rectors who give good dinners."

The final break with his wife had taken place in November 1880. He and Frances had had another of their tiresome quarrels and, in his recollection anyway, he had suggested that if she was so unhappy living at the vicarage that she could leave anytime. She agreed to do so and she said, words to the effect of, "Come along, children." He did not prevent them from getting their proper winter cloaks and caps nor did he lock them out. The "back door" to the vicarage was always open; Frances would petulantly insist on entering exclusively through the front door. It was more of her "airs." On that November day, she simply left and he had not seen her since. As for the story of how he had forced his family out to march through snowdrifts, the vicar recalled that only the briefest snow shower fell in Flitcham that day.

Inderwick did not take long to cross-examine the Rev. Mr. O'Malley. He asked the vicar, if he was innocent of all his wife had claimed, why did he then say to her, "I will beat you no longer?" O'Malley insisted he had never said any such thing. Why had he written and signed the pledge that "in the future" he would not be guilty of any violent acts? He testified that it was done only to placate his wife and the Keppels. He asked if it wasn't true that Mrs. O'Malley had once gone to the police to ask for protection from her husband. The vicar agreed that she had begun such a proceeding but had withdrawn it after consulting with him and with her family. She had acted out of a misunderstanding.

In closing for the Rev. O'Malley, Searle begged the court to understand that Bryan O'Malley and Frances Keppel had been married nine years. They had four children. Even Mrs. O'Malley did not deny that they had shared happy times. The marriage vow, however, binds a man and a woman "for better or worse." Here was a man who had struggled against the apathy and condescension of his own church to raise the money needed to restore the parish church at Flitcham and raise the lot in life of his own family and the future clergy of the village. Yet, in his own home, his wife was dissatisfied with her lot.

Arguments and clashes between two strong willed people are not unknown in married life. The allegations of personal violence had not been sufficiently proven and, therefore, Mrs. O'Malley had failed to make her legal case for a judicial separation.

It was then time for Mr. Inderwick to close for Mrs. O'Malley. It was said of the Divorce Court veteran that "a woman never knew how badly she had been treated until she had heard Inderwick address a jury on her behalf." On this occasion, however, before Inderwick could even begin to restate the case for Frances O'Malley, the foreman of the jury informed Sir James Hannen that they would not need to hear from the counsel. They had made up their minds. They had found that Mrs. Frances O'Malley had indeed been the victim of repeated acts of personal violence and was, in their opinion, deserving of the protection of a judicial separation and custody of her four children. Sir James Hannen signaled his complete agreement with the findings and issued the required court orders in conformance with the verdict. The children would remain with their mother and the Rev. Bryan O'Malley would be accorded his rightful visitation privileges. O'Malley would later ask the court to be allowed custody of his sons but the plea failed and all the children would remain with their mother.

The public airing of the bitter battles of the Rev. and Mrs. O'Malley was avidly followed in the national newspapers. *The Daily Telegraph* thought the description of the scene where the Rev. George Keppel handed the children in one door of the carriage while the Rev. O'Malley hauled them out the other side was worthy of a comic pantomime on any London stage. In reality, however, it was hardly fodder for humor but a "dismal domestic drama." The paper sharply questioned the Keppel family for failing to follow through on their earlier effort to prosecute the Rev. O'Malley in the police courts. The best thing for him would have been a good six months at hard labour.

Though embarrassed by the verdict against him and the criticism that followed him from the bench and press, the Rev. Bryan O'Malley remained the vicar of Flitcham. He soon buried his aged mother. He remained a bitter critic of the church hierarchy and their toadies.

> Very few have courage, for it requires holiness to have a sense of duty to oppose evil-doing in the hands of powerful plotters. Big people, or those in power, cannot get on without secrecy, underhand proceedings and plots; but their soul is degraded, groveling and unhappy.

His conduct became more and more eccentric as the years passed. In 1892, the duties in Flitcham were turned over to a curate-in-charge. In 1898, O'Malley was arrested for being drunk in the streets of King's Lynn. In 1899, having failed to present evidence of any willingness or intention to reform his behaviour, the Bishop of Norwich formally deprived him of his Flitcham benefice and all its (however meager) emoluments. The old Irish parson responded with yet one more blast at the Bishop and his predecessor (from the time of the earlier unpleasantness) accusing them of conspiring against a poor clergyman without power or influence. The Rev. Bryan O'Malley died in 1909. He was long outlived by Frances O'Malley who survived until 1931, passing away in her nineties.

The Rev. O'Malley had lived long enough to see – if he cared to observe – yet another restoration of old St. Mary the Virgin church in Flitcham. This time the work was funded entirely by King Edward VII – the man he had once condemned for his "sporting and frolicking."

Finally, we should note that in January 2004, Queen Elizabeth II came across the fields from Sandringham to worship at Flitcham Parish Church. What would old O'Malley have made of that?

Very Heinous Immorality

The Rev. Robert Wilson Pearse,
Rector of Gaywood

G AYWOOD IS NOW but a postcode, a community engulfed in sprawling King's Lynn. It is, nonetheless, quite an old place in its own right. In 1205, King John marched his armies north from London to subdue some rebellious barons in Norfolk. Having successfully meted out his retribution, the King halted his forces in Lynn to palaver with John Grey, the Bishop of Norwich, who had "lately erected a palace at the neighbouring village of Gaywood." The palace was well-situated. It was on just that slightly higher ground east of Lynn and enjoyed the fresh waters from the river Gay that spilled toward the Wash.

Six and a half centuries later, Gaywood was a considerable and populous village but had, to that date, managed to still elude the urban reach of King's Lynn. The newly laid tracks of the Lynn to Hunstanton railway served as an ad hoc boundary. Gaywood village was concentrated at the point where the road to Gayton divides, sending a lane north to Castle Rising, by then a moribund port on the Wash, "chiefly remarkable for its ruin." In the countryside surrounding Gaywood, the main occupations were raising cattle and sheep or farming, growing the feed grains required. Those looking for the ancient Bishop's palace were to be disappointed. It had long since been razed. Gaywood Hall now stood on the site; it was the fine home of Richard Bagge, the wealthy Lord of the Manor. Adjacent to the Hall's demesne stands the "plain cemented" church of St. Faith, Gaywood. In the 1860's, the rector in the village was the Rev. Robert Wilson Pearse.

Pearse assumed the living in Gaywood in 1854. He had enjoyed an affluent upbringing. He was the son of Brice Pearse of Ashlyns Hall, a sizeable property in Hertfordshire. His mother was the daughter of Sir Robert Williams of Penrhyn, with a fortune from coal and a comfortable long held seat in the House of Commons. Robert had been educated at Winchester and ordained upon leaving Brasenose College at Oxford. He was 26 when he first arrived in Gaywood and brought with him his new wife, the product of a marriage of the church and aristocracy. On 20 April 1854, Pearse had married Alice Wodehouse, the youngest daughter of "the Venerable" Archdeacon Charles Nourse Wodehouse, an eccentric but influential clergyman who was a canon at Norwich Cathedral. Her mother was Lady Dulcibella Hay, daughter of the 17th Earl of Errol.

The Pearse family grew rapidly, several children filling the handsome rectory. Two sons and two daughters, the youngest being Gwendoline who was born in 1866. Only a few months later, her father, the respected 39-year old rector of Gaywood was charged in an ecclesiastical court with having indecently assaulted three local youths, all "emerging into their manhood."

The conduct of the Rev. Pearse with the young lads of the village apparently had been subject for some comment prior to any formal charges. The rector was known to be a very physical man, prone to touching those he conversed with. He spent a good deal of time assisting at the national school in the village, working with the boys on their lessons. In 1866, some questions about his conduct with one of the boys led him to take some leave and absent himself from Gaywood for some period of time. However, shortly after his return, there was another incident with a shop boy in August 1867.

John Eglington was 18 and married. He worked at a shop on the Lynn Road, just west of the church. The Rev. Mr. Pearse had left some shoes to be repaired at that establishment. On the day he came to collect them, something happened in a walk-in cupboard at the shop. Young Eglington was soon claiming that the rector had "interfered" with him; Mr. Pearse claimed he had been entrapped and blackmailed. Given the earlier rumours about the rector, emotions in Gaywood were understandably excited. The churchwardens at St. Faith's felt it was only their duty to address the entire question to the Bishop. Mr. Pearse, to show the utter confidence he had in his own innocence, fully endorsed the suggestion that the Bishop be alerted to these allegations. Under the existing rules of clergy discipline in 1867, when any such "evil report" was brought to the attention of the Bishop, his Lordship was empowered to name a five-member committee of inquiry which would hear the evidence and determine whether there was "prima facie ground for further proceedings." The clerical panel assembled in Gaywood on 17 December 1867. The panel would subsequently report to the Bishop in Norwich that, unfortunately, they had determined that there were grounds for the charges made against the Rev. Pearse.

The case of *The Bishop of Norwich v. the Rev. Robert Wilson Pearse* opened in the Court of Arches on 25 May 1868 before Sir Robert Phillimore. Beyond Eglington, the promoters of the charge (i.e. the Bishop) would bring forward two additional Gaywood youths to claim they had also been subjected to the unwanted attentions of the rector. They were Matthew Monement, a shepherd, and a young groom by the name of Amis. Because these cases all involved allegations of what Phillimore called "very heinous immorality," much of the testimony was considered unfit for publication.

Amis was the first accuser to be called. The lad said he had been employed as a groom both at the rectory and at other stables in Gaywood. He had, of course, known the Rev. Pearse. There had been nothing improper in their relationship until one day, while he was alone in the harness room, the clergyman came in and began to kiss him. The simple country lad said this caught him well off guard and left him very much confused. He then, according to the redacted press coverage, "went on to describe the assault complained of." Amis admitted that he had, at first, told no one about the rector's advances. He also said that Mr. Pearse had continued to show an interest in him, though a simple stable boy, by giving him small gifts of money and visiting him in the hospital after he had been kicked by a horse.

The second lad was Matthew Monement who worked as a shepherd for a local land agent named Blake. The Monements were a family of shepherds, Matthew was one of five sons, and they resided very near Gaywood church. Matthew's story was the weakest of the three accusers. He claimed that having been a neighbour of the rector, he had often been asked to do some small chores and favours. On one occasion, Matthew told the inquiry that the rector had taken the liberty to kiss him. He was rewarded with the odd shilling. Matthew thought that Mr. Pearse had become too familiar with him. The lad, who was apparently not a tall young man, said that Mr. Pearse had frequently made comment on his height. On one occasion, the rector placed his hand on Matthew's "person" and made the quip, "I see you are small as well as short."

John Eglington, of course, was the most prominent of the trio accusing the rector. Not a groom or a shepherd, he was married and his family had long resided in Gaywood. John claimed that in August of 1867, the Rev. Pearse had come into the shop to retrieve a pair of shoes that had been left for repair. John had to go into a walk-in cupboard to get the shoes and testified that he was followed therein by the rector. The rector then closed the door behind him and began to kiss him and "otherwise indecently assaulted" him. Eglington said he was completely shocked by the clergyman's conduct and made good his escape from the cupboard. Once outside, he immediately described what had happened to him to a woman named Fysh. The cupboard incident was soon the talk of Gaywood and the ensuing "evil reports" led to the current proceedings.

The Rev. Mr. Pearse was defended by a legendary figure of the early Victorian bar, Serjeant William Ballantine. From 1848 until his retirement in 1878, Ballantine managed to figure in most of the great trials of the period – from [a rare stint as a prosecutor] the first railway murderer, Franz Muller, to the Tichborne Claimant, to his successful defense of the Gaekwar of Baroda, an Indian prince accused of attempting to poison a British agent. The grateful Gaekwar then ponied up for Ballantine the then, and longstanding, record for the highest fee. With his forensic success, he was, according to the Dictionary of National Biography, "an assiduous haunter" of clubs and taverns, an intimate of jockeys, actors and authors. A strange choice, perhaps, to defend a Norfolk clergyman.

Ballantine's reputation was, to a great extent, based on his skills in cross-examination. In his memoirs, *Some Experiences of a Barrister's Life*, he writes, "The object of cross-examination is not to produce startling effects, but to elicit facts which will support the theory intended to be put forward." With Amis, Monement and Eglington, he had pressed them on dates and seemingly trivial discrepancies. Monement, especially, was found to have difficult in keeping his story together. The others held true to their accounts.

The first witness called for the defense was Phillip Platten, the Gaywood schoolmaster; the national school in the village "having two large rooms for boys and girls." He testified that the Rev. Pearse was at the school on an almost daily basis. The rector had been a familiar figure at the school and was much loved by all the children. Mr. Platten had never known or even suspected that the rector had ever behaved improperly toward any of the male youths at the school. One of the three accusers, Matthew Monement, had been dismissed from the school as a trouble-maker.

Mrs. Robert Pearse, the rector's wife was called. She described her husband as an effusive man who loved children. He was animated in conversation, often placing his hand on the other person. She insisted that her husband's brief absence from Gaywood in 1866 had not been related to any suggestions of improprieties with a local youth. She tearfully concluded that she was confident that all the charges against her husband were untrue.

At this point, Mr. Ballantine made the unusual request that he be allowed to present the Rev. Robert Wilson Pearse as a witness. While it is now taken as a given that a defendant may take the witness stand – in 1868, the accused had no right to testify. JP Deane, the counsel for the Bishop of Norwich, objected. Sir Robert Phillimore overruled the objection and, in a precedent setting action, allowed Ballantine to call his client into the box.

Mr. Pearse took the stand and provided the court with his biographical details, for the record. He had been married for fourteen years and had four children. He did, in fact, know all three of the young men arrayed against him. As for Amis, the rector stated that he knew him as the groom employed by his neighbour. He had never been alone with the lad in a harness room or anywhere else. He had occasionally seen the lad in the roads and footpaths around Gaywood. He had never kissed him. He had never committed any indecent assaults on the young man. Pearse conceded that he had stopped in to visit Amis after the lad had been injured, but, the rector argued, that is hardly out of the routine for any clergyman.

Mr. Pearse knew Matthew Monement very well as the family also lived very near the rectory. Matthew frequently did small errands for the rector and was often rewarded with a few pence. Mr. Pearse said he was a man, as his wife had testified, who talked with his hands, touching and gesticulating. He had chided Matthew as to the lad's lack of stature but insisted he had only touched the boy's chest whilst he made the innocent, if mischaracterized, remark, "You are small as well as short." There had never been anything improper in his relationship with Matthew. He had never kissed the lad, touched his person or otherwise assaulted him.

Finally, the questions came around to the most serious allegation involving John Eglington. The lad had been seen coming out of a cupboard with the clergyman and the youth had immediately and publicly accused him of "interfering with him." The Rev. Pearse said the cupboard incident had occurred but in a way entirely different from that as described by young Eglington. The rector had gone to Eglington's shop to pick up shoes left for repair. When he entered the shop, there was no one about. He called out and, suddenly, from a cupboard, Eglington "popped out." Thinking the youth was acting rather furtively, Pearse recalled that he suggested, at first jokingly, that Eglington was hiding something or someone in the cupboard. He asked the lad, "What's going on in there?" He then took a step or two inside to see for himself when Eglington came in behind him and locked the cupboard door. The rector testified that Eglington began threatening him with exposure for unnatural offences unless he paid him for his silence. The shop-lad vowed to tell everyone how the rector had assaulted him. Mr. Pearse said Eglington told him that his father knew a case where a man had been accused of the same thing and had been transported for twenty years and the same would happen to him if he didn't pay up. Pearse said he became distraught and begged to know why Eglington wanted to ruin him and disgrace his wife and children. The rector then begged to be released from the cupboard. When he did make his escape, he was followed outside by Eglington. Mrs. Fysh was in the shop and the lad told the (no doubt startled) woman what he claimed had just happened. According to Pearse, that same night, Eglington and his father came to the rectory. The elder man demanded an explanation for his conduct with his son. Pearse said he told Eglington that his son was telling a lie and was attempting to extort money from him. And, he knew where his son had gotten the idea, from his father. He then demanded that the Eglingtons, *pere et fils*, leave the rectory immediately. From the witness box, in a firm voice, on his oath as a clergyman and a married man and father, the Rev. Mr. Pearse swore that his was the true and only complete account of the cupboard incident.

The prosecuting counsel, Mr. Deane, did not use much of his time to challenge the Rev. Pearse's version of the events involving the young men Amis, Monement and Eglington. Instead, he opened a line of questioning about an incident in the rector's past involving a boy who had been coming to the clergyman preparing for his confirmation. This, of course, is the risk a defense counsel must take when placing a client in the box. There is no way of knowing where the prosecuting barrister will take the questioning. Mr. Pearse admitted that there had been rumours current in the village about the time of the boy's preparation for the sacrament but he had he not behaved improperly with that un-named lad. He conceded that he was aware that at the time the boy's mother had made comments about the rector and her son but no case was ever made out of it, for lack of evidence. Rev. Pearse insisted that then, as with these current charges, it was a false accusation.

In his closing comments to the Dean of Arches, Mr. Ballantine said the case against the Rev. Robert Wilson Pearse rested on nothing more than circumstantial evidence. It was freely admitted by the rector that he had met with these youths. What of that? Gaywood was not then a large community. He had reason to be at Eglington's shop. Amis and Monement were workers employed near the rectory who often helped him, a busy clergyman, with errands, etc. Though the meetings could be proven, the details and dates – especially with Monement's evidence – were not as verifiable. Ballantine stressed that, most importantly, none of the three lads could provide any corroborative proof of the horrific conduct they alleged against Mr. Pearse. The rector, continued Ballantine, no doubt had a familiar way of acting with boys but it was one that was not inconsistent with purity of intentions. Would the schoolmaster have come forward to testify that the clergyman was at the school almost daily? Would he have welcomed him amongst the children under his supervision had he feared the man's appetites were so loathsome?

Phillimore interrupted to ask Ballantine what motive had these three simple young men to invent such a serious and awful charge? Ballantine could probably have answered, "I was getting to that, m'Lord," before making the case for blackmail. Young Eglington, once he had successfully entrapped the rector in the shop cupboard, had plainly stated that he knew of a man charged with similar crimes who had been transported across the sea. The implicit suggestion was to pay up or lies would be told. Eglington and his father went to the rectory that night, not out of concern for the rector's behaviour, but to extort money. They had hoped that the rector would pay for his silence. He would not. Young Eglington had then recruited two simple village lads to concoct their stories of additional incidents.

Why, instead, did Eglington or his angry father not go to the police? Parliament had only just (in 1861) ended the death penalty for buggery. However, "an indecent assault upon any male person" was still a misdemeanour punished with jail and hard labour.

Ballantine then concluded, with emotion appropriate to moment, reminding the court of the presence throughout this ordeal of the loyal wife of the rector, Mrs. Alice Pearse. Her father was a respected Archdeacon in the Cathedral in Norwich; imagine her personal shame as the very Bishop of Norwich her father had so faithfully served was now accusing her husband of the most abhorrent conduct. Yet, she answered all the questions put to her firmly, defending her husband magnificently. Is it even possible that a respected, married clergyman with a family, and the youngest child but two years old, could be guilty of such reprehensible behaviour? Surely not, concluded Ballantine, on the flimsiest evidence of the three plotters who had made the charges under investigation.

Mr. Deane rose to conclude for the prosecution, asking first that he be allowed to say that the choice of requiring the presence of Mrs. Pearse to attend before such an inquiry, with the subject matter as offensive as possible, had not been his. Mr. Ballantine had called her as a witness. That her situation was a very painful one was plain to everyone who had been part of the inquiry. Nonetheless, these charges were as serious as could be imagined and however difficult the task might be, the Bishop of Norwich must prosecute with vigour. Deane said it was certainly clear that the case against the rector of Gaywood had been proven. The young men had told their stories and withstood the cross-examination of one of England's finest barristers. There was no proof of any cabal on their part. The suspicions held by many residents of the parish about their rector had far preceded the cases made by these lads. Mr. Pearse and his curious behaviour around young men had been often remarked upon. What business had the Rev. Pearse visiting a stable lad in the hospital? Why would he touch the body of Matthew Monement? As Mr. Phillimore could see with his own eyes, the Rev. Mr. Pearse was a man much larger than young Eglington. Can it possibly be accepted that the slight youth of seventeen was able to force the clergyman – a man of nearly forty - into a cupboard and keep him there?

Mr. Deane also declared that, regardless of the outcome of the case before the Dean of Arches, an appeal would be raised on the issue of the decision to permit the Rev. Pearse to testify in his defense. The so-called "doctrine of incompetency" was then the rule in all English courtrooms, criminal and civil. Basically, it was accepted that the testimony of any accused person is, at root, worthless because what else would a reasonable judge or jury expect but that the defendant would deny whatever wrongdoing is at issue. In a way, this doctrine also served to protect the accused from the criticism if the decision was made *not to testify*. What – the other side would bray - are they afraid of? That question could not be asked if the defendant had no right to enter the witness box at all.

After two days of testimony, the proceedings adjourned on 26 May 1868. The ruling was issued ten days later. On 4 June 1868, Sir Robert Phillimore began, to the excruciating discomfiture of the Rev. Mr. Pearse, with a rather lengthy defense of his decision to permit the defendant to give evidence. Before him was the case of a clergyman of the established church. He allowed that the Rev. Pearse certainly had the "strongest motives" to deny the charges against him. Given the presumption that a man in such a revered and trusted profession would always tell the truth, Sir Robert admitted it was reasonable to ask if it was not unfair to those who had brought these charges against him? He felt, however, that any clergyman who could consider engaging in such "various abominations" had so "defiled his conscience" that the additional sin of perjury could not be ruled out. Therefore, the Rev. Pearse must be treated as any other witness – listened to and observed carefully to establish his credibility. He concluded that the decision was based on fairness:

> The extreme hardship, I should say injustice, of allowing a clerk [a clergyman was a "clerk in holy orders"] to be accused of any offence, however infamous, alleged to have been committed in the presence of the accuser alone and supported by his testimony alone, and of sealing up the mouth of the accused, who, if innocent, may give a satisfactory refutation of the charge, and, if guilty, ought not to be protected by a technical rule from exposure, more especially in a case where third parties, the parishioners, have a right to demand that the cure of their souls shall not be entrusted to a wicked pastor.

Now, back to the peculiar familiarities of the rector of Gaywood. Phillimore said that he had closely observed the three young men who had given evidence against the Rev. Pearse. He found the groom Amis to be a straightforward and honest lad who gave his evidence and held to his story. Monement was more problematical with numerous errors in detail having been brought out by Mr. Ballantine. However, as other witnesses had given enough supporting testimony, Monement's version of events could not be automatically discounted. The lead accuser was young Eglington. The Dean of Arches was impressed by Mr. Deane's argument as to the relative size of the clergyman and the shop-boy. Mr. Pearse was so much the larger man in stature that his claim to have been over-powered and locked in the cupboard and forced to listen to false accusations cannot be accepted. The rector's curious "familiarity" with young men was well known though not on its face anything proving guilt. However, visiting a servant boy in the hospital, touching others, etc reasonably raised concerns. Most damaging, perhaps, thought Phillimore was the previous incident involving the Rev. Pearse with the confirmation boy.

> The defendant was, by his own confession, guilty of an impru-
> dence so grave as to create suspicion, however unjust, that he
> had offended in the very manner he was now accused.

It must be remembered, of course, that the evidence of this separate case was only elicited from Rev. Pearse because of Mr. Ballantine's decision to call him as a witness and Phillimore's ruling to permit it. It had proven damning.

Sir Robert Phillimore concluded that, "by the reasons of common sense and the principles of justice," the charges against the Rev. Pearse had been "substantially proven." Undoubtedly, this was a decision that would bring great pain and loss of position to a married man with a large family. From the bench, however, Sir Robert declared, "I am not at liberty to indulge any feelings of private compassion for the distress this decision might cause." These were not isolated incidents; the testimony had shown the conduct had even preceded these latest acts. "Evil reports" had been circulated in Gaywood for some time. Because of the Rev. Robert Wilson Pearse's "repeated acts of this peculiar obscenity," no punishment short of the ultimate would be acceptable. He must be deprived of the rectory of Gaywood "and all of its emoluments, etc."

The Rev. Mr. Pearse mounted a last appeal before the Privy Council in London. The verdict in the Court of Arches was attacked on two grounds. It was claimed, perhaps with reason, that the decision to arraign the rector on all three charges at once was unjust. It made what were individually flimsy claims appear to be part of a pattern of what Sir Robert Phillimore could characterize as "repeated acts." Secondly, the rector's new counsel argued that Serjeant Ballantine had failed to make an appropriately compelling argument that the clergyman was being blackmailed. It was said that Ballantine – who had taken his fee and moved on, he rarely did appeals – had not articulated sufficiently the seriousness of the demand for "hush money" from Eglington. The appeal suggested that the Rev. Pearse had been the victim of a plot orchestrated by "dirty minds in the village of Gaywood."

Sir James Wilde delivered the brief ruling for the Privy Council, dismissing the appeal. Sir James said that the point as to separating the charges was an interesting one but it had not been made before Sir Robert Phillimore when it should have been put forward. As for the blackmail allegations, these had been raised fully in the Court of Arches. Neither issue, however, concluded Wilde was of such merit as to have changed the verdict owing to the "evidence of so filthy and horrible a character."

A new rector took up his duties at St. Faith's in Gaywood; the Rev. R.A. Whalley would remain there into the 1900's. The Pearses left the town but not together. After the trial and the disgrace of her husband having been convicted of "heinous immorality," Mrs. Pearse had gone home to her mother. Accompanied by her two daughters, Mrs. Pearse was living in Lowestoft on the Marine Parade with Mrs. Dulcibella Wodehouse. The wife of the one-time rector of Gaywood survived until 1914.

The Rev. Mr. Pearse, meantime, had also gone home to his widowed mother in Bayswater. As late as 1891, he was still living at 9 Hyde Park Street, joined then by his unmarried brother. The Rev. Robert Wilson Pearse died in Thanet in Kent in 1897.

John Eglington remained in Gaywood. In 1881, he had prospered to the status of "general merchant" on the Lynn Road.

Would It Surprise You To Know?

The Rev. Alfred W.L. Rivett, Rector of Clippesby.

A FTER A clerical career of nearly forty years including a decade in the African veldt, the Rev. William Alfred Lovely Rivett was hoping to end his ministerial service as a rector someplace quiet in his native Norfolk. In 1898, he was therefore delighted to accept the living in Clippesby, a village but nine miles northwest of Yarmouth, where the clergyman was born in 1836. Clippesby's ancient Church of St. Peter was another of those round-towered churches so peculiar to East Anglia. Arriving with him at the rectory in Clippesby was Anna Mary, his wife of forty years. They had no children.

Clippesby seemed perfect: there were hardly more than a hundred residents. The census shows the locals were almost exclusively farmers, cowkeepers and the like. The only local gentry had been the Musketts, the family that provided the rectors in Clippesby for most of the century. The Musketts had resided at Clippesby House, a "handsome mansion of white brick standing on rising ground with commanding prospects." The last Rev. Muskett had died there the previous year and the house was now vacant and for sale. The Rivetts went about settling in amongst their new rustic flock.

Whatever wishes the old cleric may have had for a peaceful time of it, they were soon to be dashed. The post would arrive in Clippesby at eight each morning from Yarmouth. One morning in early April of 1898, every house and cottage in the village received an anonymous postcard. The message on the card was certain to cause comment:

> Would it surprise you to know that your rector, the Rev. William Lovely Rivett, is not a person of the highest moral character? Rumour has it that, while at Norwich, a maid-servant of his had a child, of which he, although a married man, was the father, and it is a positive fact that a servant in his employ drowned herself at Norwich.

Even (presumably literate) cow-keepers will talk and it was obvious that the Rev. Mr. Rivett could not ignore these sensational allegations against him. Who could have written such a thing?

Inquiries were launched by the Rev. Mr. Rivett's solicitor. The sender was easily traced, in fact, he had taken little effort, it seems, to cover his tracks. Though unsigned, the cards had all been postmarked in Norwich. A postal employee had recognized the cards as having been sold to Thomas Richard Berger Wilson, a 38-year old clerk with the Norwich Union Fire Office, an insurance firm in Surrey Street. When Wilson was contacted and threatened with prosecution unless he withdrew these libelous charges, he responded defiantly. He had no intention of recanting a single word that he had written and he informed Mr. Rivett's solicitor that he had taken the additional step of sending the same postcard to the Bishop of Norwich. Wilson's note contained a new threat, "You may inform your client that if he inserts a bogus apology in any paper I shall have to make a further report on him." At that point, the police were called in and Wilson was arrested and jailed to await the upcoming assizes. The charge against him was "unlawfully and maliciously publishing certain defamatory libels of and concerning" the Rev. William Alfred Lovely Rivett.

Postcard libels were not uncommon and clergymen were frequently their victims. In fact, only weeks before the Rev. Rivett's ordeal, another Norfolk clergyman, the Rev. Alan Gwyn Blyth of Heigham, had been targeted. Apparently a female Sunday School teacher, distraught over Mr. Blyth's recent marriage, sent postcards addressed to his wife as "Miss Edith Moule, care of the Rev. A.G. Blyth." The woman had also disrupted services at Heigham church. She was clearly unbalanced.

As for Mr. Rivett, it will be helpful here to briefly recapitulate that reverend gentleman's career. Born in Yarmouth, the son of a baker, Rivett had gone out to South Africa as a youth. He was just twenty when he married Anna Mary Saunderson in Pietermaritzburg in 1856. He was 20 and she was 35. According to *Crockford's Clerical Directory*, Rivett was ordained in Natal in 1859 and served under the controversial Bishop Colenso. He was assigned to Durban and remembered there as a "worthy and hard-working" churchman. He and his wife left Africa for England in 1865. Somehow he managed to write a book about those six years entitled *Ten Years Church Work in Natal*. But no matter that.

He returned to Great Yarmouth as a curate, following that appointment with similar short stays in Bunnell and New Buckenham. In 1871, the Rev. Mr. Rivett was made rector of St. Martin's, Palace Plain, the small church wedged between the Cathedral and the river Wensum in Norwich. He would be there for fourteen years. The church was unfortunately hard by the giant British Gas Works, just across the river, and infamous for their "pestiferous emanations." Nonetheless, Mr. Rivett's stay at St. Martin's was an eventful one; he presided over some extensive renovations including the restoration of the west tower to its original height. A man who enjoyed liturgical music, he improved the church organ by the addition of "a swell and pedal pipes." St. Martin's was soon known across Norwich for "a full choral service each Sunday evening with a large and surpliced choir." The postcard author, Thomas Richard Berger Wilson, was a member of that choir at St. Martin's.

We must presume there was a close relationship between the rector and young Wilson. Not necessarily a romantic one as Wilson made no such claim. Certainly, if he had he made such a charge, he would have also implicated himself. Hence, it cannot be ruled out. Mr. Rivett was almost fifty; his wife was now in her sixties. There were no children. Perhaps, the impetus for the relationship came from Wilson. In 1885, when Rivett announced he was moving to Barnstaple, Wilson was devastated. Rivett curiously encouraged the young man to get married. Again, this suggests the young man's affection for his parson was a matter of some concern. Before leaving, Rivett also helped Wilson find a good job. All of this does show a level of interest on Rivett's part beyond what he could afford to offer to every member of his "large surpliced choir."

In 1885, the Rev. Mr. Rivett left Norwich – and the stricken Wilson – and took up his duties as vicar of the Church of St. Mary Magdalene in Barnstaple, Devon. He served there twelve years – apparently without incident - until the Clippesby vacancy called him back to Norfolk. Now, in his early sixties, the Rev. Mr. Rivett, after a quarter-century of running busy "town" churches, had expressed his wish to slow down. The rectory at remote Clippesby seemed the ideal "last post." Then the morning post arrived.

The case against Thomas Wilson was to be heard at the Norfolk Assizes at the Shirehall in Norwich on 20 June 1898. Presiding was the irascible giant of the late Victorian bench, Justice Sir Henry Hawkins. The Hall was especially crowded but the attraction was not the "Clippesby Postcard Case." The great bulk of the attention was drawn to the trial of George Watt for "The Sprowston Murder." Watt's wife had left him saying she wanted a "better husband." He tracked her down and shot her three times at close range. He then spent several hours at a series of pubs, drinking until the police caught up with him. Watt's insanity plea was to mean a lengthy trial and Hawkins wanted to get the postcard case out of the way. That seemed very likely with the announcement that Wilson was to plead guilty.

Wilson, joined by his counsel Thomas Blofeld, stood before Justice Hawkins. The defendant was asked if he was the man who "on or about 31 March 1898" had mailed these libelous postcards to the residents of Clippesby? Wilson replied, "I am sorry to say I am, sir." Mr. Blofeld came from a clerical background; his father and brother were clergymen, his mother and wife were the daughters of clergymen. He told Justice Hawkins that his client now wished to "unreservedly withdraw every imputation" and by his plea make clear there was "absolutely no foundation" for any of the charges. However, the attorney said that he was certain that the Rev. Mr. Rivett enjoyed such a lofty standing in Norwich, and in his new village of Clippesby, that these libelous charges would, he trusted, do him no harm. "Not a shadow of a shade of suspicion," should fall upon the reverend gentleman's reputation.

Blofeld told Sir Henry that Wilson was the son of an Inland Revenue agent. The Wilson family had worshipped at St. Martin's Palace Plain during the latter years of the clergyman's tenure there. Then a lad in his late teens, Thomas had been a member of the church's acclaimed choir and had also served as a "superintendent" of the Sunday School programs. He was a very sensitive and nervous youth and when Mr. Rivett left Norwich for Barnstaple, Wilson was greatly disappointed, indeed upset. Mr. Rivett had done his best by the youth, using his connections to attain for Wilson a post with the Norwich Union Fire Office, where the defendant was still employed. He had also urged him to find a young woman and get married and raise a family. The defendant now had a young wife and infant child. There had been no contact between Thomas Wilson and the Rev. Mr. Rivett in the thirteen years since the rector had left for Devon. For some reason, however, Wilson had conceived the opinion that he was being watched and the watchers had been set upon him by the Rev. Mr. Rivett. At that point, Justice Hawkins – looking perhaps to accelerate matters – suggested that Wilson might best be dispatched to a lunacy asylum. Was that Mr. Blofeld's intent, to plead insanity? Blofeld said Wilson's delusions were "not as bad as that, my Lord" but he did wish to call witnesses on his client's behalf.

John Messent, Wilson's employer at the insurance agency, said the defendant was a good worker but very reclusive. He had told co-workers of his sense that he was always being watched. The only other witness was Ellen Wilson, Thomas' wife. *The Eastern Daily Press* observer said she appeared to be in "a half-fainting condition." Mrs. Wilson said her husband had been "strange" for some time. She thought her husband was a troubled man but he knew he had done wrong; all she asked for now was for Thomas to be released and free to go home with his wife and child.

Ernest Wild QC was prosecuting the case for the Crown, acting on behalf of the victim, the Rev. Mr. Rivett. Wild said that the Rector of Clippesby was willing to forgive his former young friend in return for the retraction and apology that had been proffered. For the record, however, Wild wished to address the charges contained in the postcards. In fact, a servant at the rectory of St. Martin, Palace Plain, had drowned during the years the Rev. Mr. Rivett was at that church. That case had been fully investigated and an inquest determined the unfortunate woman's death was accidental. She was not pregnant at the time of her death, nor had she ever had a relationship with or a child by the Rev. Mr. Rivett. Those were the facts of the case. The Bishop of Norwich was fully apprised of the case and no church enquiry was thought necessary. Mr. Rivett had served fourteen respected years in Norwich, twelve more in Barnstaple, and wished now only to live out his years in peace in Clippesby.

Hawkins, the murder case pressing and an anticipatory crowd no doubt growing restive, said he would have to think the matter over before pronouncing sentence. However much Mr. Rivett may be willing to forgive, the justice said the public must be protected from such outrageous libels. Libels sent via postcards that can be read by anyone, were especially malicious. First the Blyth case and now this; examples must be set. He ordered the parties to return after the Sprowston case was finished. Thomas R.B. Wilson, in the meantime, was returned to his cell.

The Sprowston trial lasted several long days. Despite sweltering late June heat, Justice Hawkins refused to allow windows to be opened in Shirehall. The trial ended with a guilty verdict and the always emotional ritual of donning the "black cap" when Justice Hawkins pronounced the death sentence. The convicted killer was led away to his doom. Thomas Wilson was brought forward. It was not a propitious time for him to decide to withdraw his guilty plea.

"What?" roared Justice Hawkins. Wilson, in a highly excited and rambling speech, denounced his own attorney, Mr. Blofeld. The accused said he had been led into a trap and misled. For several weeks he had been held in jail, "herded with creatures of the lowest grade of humanity." He knew that his guilty plea would result in a sentence that would return him to a confinement that he could not endure. His wife and infant child would be without him and his earnings. He could not face it. Moreover, it was all cruelly unfair for he was telling the truth, every word of it. He must be allowed to call witnesses who would support the charges he had made against the Rev. Mr. Rivett.

Hawkins warned Wilson to take care. Mr. Blofeld was a respected and experienced counsel and his advice to plead guilty was wise. To tear up that plea now would only make matters much worse for Wilson. The defendant tearfully begged for time to find witnesses to support his charges.

Hawkins had heard enough.

> You have considerably aggravated the charges against you. Instead of apologizing to the man you have wantonly assaulted, you have repeated the wicked suggestions against him. Your learned counsel has given you good advice. You have now thrown away the good effect in persisting in these statements.

Hawkins declared that under these changed circumstances, he would not agree to Rev. Mr. Rivett's gracious request for mercy. He sentenced Thomas Wilson to a year in jail and the trembling man was led back to the cells.

Hawkins left Norwich, the assizes completed. *The Eastern Daily Press*, whose correspondents were forced to endure several sweltering breezeless days at Shirehall, bid him a welcome adieu. "It may perhaps be admitted that if Time has lengthened his days, it has also tended to curtail his patience." In his two decades on the criminal bench, Hawkins had earned the nickname "'Anging 'Arry 'Awkins." *The Dictionary of National Biography*, however, contended:

> The alliterative attractiveness of the phrase gave rise to a loose popular impression that he was a judge of a peculiarly severe or even savage temper. For this idea there was no real foundation.

It may be presumed that Thomas Wilson was not consulted when those words were written.

The Rev. Mr. Rivett returned to Clippesby, his reputation salvaged. His wife Anna Mary predeceased him in 1910. He did get his wish, ending his days as rector at St. Peter's. *The Times* took notice of his death, "He died at his rectory on Monday 3 Dec 1917 having been stricken following services the previous day."

There Was Something Rotten in the State of Burnham

The Rev. F.W. Waldron,
Curate of Burnham Market

THE REV Frederick William Waldron, the curate to the Rev. William Bates of the parish church in Burnham Market, was known to occasionally delight in the opportunity to display a rather advanced view on human sexuality. Over dinner one night at the rectory, the Rev. Mr. Bates had expressed his disapproval of the general laxity of morals in village society. No doubt, the rector was shocked when his curate replied, in words to the effect, "Dear Bates, you worry too much about such things. Everybody does it." Mr. Waldron might have thought, as well, that his rector was a hypocrite. For the curate had just written to a parishioner, "Who in Burnham does not believe that he is living in abominable sin?" What in the world was going on here?

Our story begins in 1854. The Rev. William Bates DD had been the rector in Burnham Market (then also known as Burnham Westgate) for only a few years. He was the son of a wealthy Northumberland colliery owner. Educated at Cambridge, he had spent a dozen years there as a fellow of Christ's College. The living at St. Mary's, Burnham Market, was under the patronage of that college and in 1849, Bates came to the pleasantly situated village as the new rector. In addition to St. Mary's, the new rector would also be responsible for two other churches in nearby villages, St. Margaret's at Burnham Norton and All Saints at Burnham Sutton and Ulph. To assist with these liturgical duties in "the Burnhams," Mr. Waldron was employed as a curate in 1852.

Burnham Market in the 1850's – as it is, of course, today – was a very pretty village. Holkham Hall, the seat of the Earl of Leicester was nearby and it was just two miles to the "fine and extensive sea-sands at Burnham Overy Staithe." The village may have been quite pleasant: the old church at the west end of the market place was less salubrious. The visitor who prepared the entry in the contemporary Norfolk directory had concluded: "The clerestory window is perfect but otherwise the structure is old, the walls are damp, and the monuments are of no great interest."

The Rev. Dr. Bates would see to that. He promptly sued his patrons, claiming that the Fellows of Christ's College, Cambridge were shorting him the tithe money required to improve the church. It was a lengthy and, it must be said, tedious dispute involving moeities and arcane, sadly ill-defined deeds. The dispute unfortunately became a heated one and the Rev. Bates was threatened with legal action over some of his comments. He had quickly gotten the reputation as a hot-headed and litigious man.

Rev. Bates had come from Cambridge to Burnham Market, just past the age of forty and single. In a way, that was for the best, because a married clergyman with a family would have come to Burnham Market and discovered there was no suitable rectory. The Rev. Dr. Bates would see to that as well. In 1853, he began construction on a handsome new rectory, in the Elizabethan style, on a plot of higher ground just west of the church. In the meantime, the curate, Mr. Waldron, was consigned to find a room in the village. The National School in Burnham Market, built in 1836, and with 55 boys and 80 girls in daily attendance, had recently been expanded. The new addition provided more classroom space plus, on the upper floors, "convenient residences for the teachers." The curate took his lodgings therein.

Rev. F.W. Waldron was in his early 30's, born in Scotland and also a Cantab, having left St. John's College with a record for outstanding abilities in mathematics. After tutoring the sons of an Admiral, he began his clerical career as a navy chaplain, seeing Pacific service aboard the HMS

Amazon. Seeking employment on land, he had been employed by the Rev. Mr Bates at Burnham. He was also unmarried. Though he lodged at the school with the teachers, Mr. Burr and the widowed Mrs. Childs, he was frequently asked to dine with the rector. The relationship between the two clergymen had been an amicable one until some friction arose in the fall of 1854. Mr. Bates had been called away and Waldron was left for some six weeks to handle all the parish duties. He had – rightly or wrongly – expected additional compensation for these extra duties. However, the Rev. Bates, at least in Mr. Waldron's opinion, had too curtly dashed those hopes. A decided frost came over their relationship. Waldron thought it was time to seek a more remunerative position. Therefore, neither gentleman could legitimately feign unhappiness when Mr. Waldron accepted an offer to become the headmaster at a small school in Leicestershire. The two clergymen had a final dinner together on a November evening; it was on that occasion, that the Rev. Bates would recall that he had been so taken aback by his curate's flippant comment about marital incontinence.

If statistics do matter, Mr. Waldron had a good argument. At least in rural Norfolk - there was much to support his bawdy conclusion. In 1850, only four years before our story took place, a series of unsigned "Letters from Rural Districts" appeared in *The Morning Chronicle* in London. Writing from Norfolk, the "special correspondent" solemnly declared, "there appears to be a complete want of decency among the people." The bastardy rate was at 53%. Regardless, it was probably for the best that Mr. Waldron was leaving Burnham Market.

Nonetheless, one can only assume that it was a heavy blow that fell upon the Rev. Mr. Bates in early December when he learned that a former housemaid at the teacher's residence was pregnant and she named the Rev. F. W. Waldron as the father. Louisa Johnson was just a girl of seventeen. Making matters even worse for the Rev. Bates, the pregnancy had been discovered soon after the young woman had gone down to London to be a housemaid for the rector's brother. Thomas Bates QC had recently lost his wife in childbirth and had asked his brother if a village girl might be found to join his household.

Louisa had come highly recommended – by none other than the departing Rev. F. W. Waldron. But, soon after Louisa's arrival in London, her *enceinte* condition became obvious to Thomas Bates and the girl tearfully confessed her fall to him. Bates immediately wrote to his brother and informed him of his curate's profligacy, declaring, "The scoundrel must go to the dogs. And her too!" Louisa was soon packed off back to Burnham Market, expecting.

Mr. Bates knew immediately that he would have to communicate the intelligence of this outrage - upon an innocent village girl - to Mr. Waldron's new employers. He wrote to the trustees of the Sedley School:

> Gentleman, I am now in possession of irrefragable proof of the exceeding wickedness of Mr. Waldron's character, and I call upon you in the name of all that is holy and good, to dismiss him instantly from the mastership of your school.

The rector included the full details of the story of seduction and abandonment on the part of the man they had honoured by appointing as their new headmaster.

In addition, Mr. Bates wrote privately to his erstwhile curate to inform him that, as his former rector, he could do no less than place the entire matter in the hands of the Bishop of Norwich:

> The whole of your abominable wickedness is now revealed, and as I am sure that your heart, principles and conduct are thoroughly bad, and that you will never have the grace to repent, I advise you at once to abscond and hide yourself where you will never be heard of more.

Such a charge could not stand unchallenged. On the 27th of March 1855, at the Norwich Assizes, the Rev. Mr. Waldron sued the Rev. William Bates, rector of Burnham Market, for libel and put in a claim for damages in the amount of £1000. The Rev. Mr. Bates answered not guilty to the charge, insisting that he had simply stated the truth: his former curate "debauched and carnally knew a young girl then living in his service." The Lord Chief Baron Pollock would preside over this regrettable imbroglio.

Mr. Serjeant Byles was to represent the accused curate. To prove the publication of the libel, i.e., the letter sent to the trustees at the school, Mr. Henry Needham was called to the stand. Needham was the chief trustee of the Sedley School, endowed in the 1630's by Sir John Sedley "for all the poor boys of the parish" in Wymondham, Leicestershire. He testified that the decision to hire Mr. Waldron had been based, in great measure, on "very commendatory" letters from the Rev. Mr. Bates. At Sedley, the new headmaster had been doing quite well. If the charges were found to be true, it would mean, of course, that Waldron could not remain in the position. Needham said that he had summoned Waldron immediately after receiving the letter from Burnham Market. The trustee testified that Waldron had vehemently denied being intimate with Louisa Johnson in any way. He swore that he was not the father of her child and it was all a plot, on her part, to extort money from him. Needham said that the trustees had given the matter a great deal of thought, and it was decided that Mr. Waldron's explanation had been sincere and honest. The trustee said that he wrote back to the Rev. Bates suggesting that he was mistaken. When Bates persisted more energetically in his accusations, Needham ended the exchange with a rather sharp reply:

> We decline any further correspondence with you. A gentleman, a neighbour of your own, states that you have been twice convicted of slander, and therefore we feel that it matters little what you say of anyone. The trustees have appointed Mr. Waldron and they will not be moved by your insinuations. It is only a pity that you don't have a spark of the holiness which you so invoke.

Mr. Bates did not deny writing the letters to the Sedley trustees. It would then be his responsibility to prove that the charges he had made against Mr. Waldron were true or that he *honestly believed* them to be true. Truth was a justification for libel but only when the publication of the "truth" could be shown to have a public benefit. It was surely of public interest that a clergyman – facing this disgraceful charge – currently held the position of headmaster in a historically endowed school. Harris Prendergast was the counsel for Mr. Bates and he told the jury that it would be his task to present damning evidence proving that the former curate had seduced this village housemaid and, to make matters worse, if possible, he had "recourse to violence to gratify his passions."

The first witness called to the stand was Louisa Johnson. The young woman gave her age as seventeen and said she had given birth to a baby boy in February of that year. The father of that child was, she stated in a firm voice, the Rev. F.W. Waldron, the former curate of Burnham Market. Her testimony, as reported in the press, was filled with elisions, obscuring the more salacious contents from the eyes of those more sensitive readers. Louisa said she was a servant at the national school and had a room in the teacher's residence on the same floor as Mr. Waldron. They would, as was perfectly acceptable in the situation, exchange passing pleasantries from time to time. She said, however, Mr. Waldron had begun to press his attentions on her. For instance, as she walked down the hall, he would stand in his doorway and beg her to come in for a kiss. On one occasion, when she was sewing a button on for him, he pulled her down on to his knee where he thought she would be more comfortable. He asked her impertinent questions, such as, how high were her garters? Louisa said she had repeatedly asked the Rev. Mr. Waldron to behave in a more respectful manner towards her. She thought herself fully capable of resisting him until an occasion around Christmas time in 1853 when he forcibly had his way with her on a couch.

Louisa related how the curate had told her that she could never tell anyone about what had happened. The people wouldn't believe her word against a clergyman's and she would surely lose her position and have to leave Burnham Market. She testified that, after that first lovemaking, Mr. Waldron declared that she was now his. He used to come into her room and sleep with her most nights, when possible. He talked of someday getting married when he was able to support a wife on something more than a curate's pay. Then, she was stunned when he announced he was leaving for his new school in Leicestershire and she was not going to go with him but instead she was to be sent to London. On the 19th of November, she wrote to Mr. Waldron:

> Have arrived safely … after a journey filled with tears and sadness. Till then I never knew the loss of a friend. Dear master whose servant she hoped to be again, who had taught her many things, she should never be able to thank sufficiently.

Once in London, however, now residing with the Thomas Bates family, she soon realized that she was pregnant. Louisa wrote again to Mr. Waldron on the 20th of December:

> Sir I am about to inform you of the troubles you have drove me to for I am with child. … As you have brought me to these trials, you must help me through them. I shall hope to hear from you and receive some relief.

He had not deigned to reply.

Cross-examined by Byles, counsel for Mr. Waldron, Louisa conceded that the curate had been quite kind to her – otherwise. She had never complained to the rector about Mr. Waldron's behaviour. Though her parents had a cottage very near to her lodgings, she had never raised the issue with them either. She explained that her parents were quite poor and she couldn't go home to them; she would have to wrestle with this problem herself. Literally. She had only discussed Mr. Waldron's pursuit of her with the head teacher Mrs. Childs but she had never told anyone that she was his lover. Referring again to her letters, Byles suggested, since her child was born in February, she must have known she was pregnant in November. Yet, she did not mention it in her first letter to Mr. Waldron from London. Louisa did not have an answer.

In any case of this type, it was to be expected that defending counsel would bring before the jury the names of any other men who might have been intimate with the accuser. The gentlemen of the jury must be made to wonder how innocent, anyway, was this Norfolk housemaid? Byles wanted to know more about Louisa's friendship with a lad in the village by the name of Norris, a cart-maker's apprentice. She admitted that she had told a friend, another local girl, Polly Grix, that Norris had given her some presents. Nothing too grand; after all, an apprentice could not afford much. Trinkets from the local fair, and the like. She denied, however, that she had ever "walked out" with young Norris. When asked if she had ever told anyone that she liked Norris, Louisa declared, "I hated him!"

Mrs. Caroline Childs was the next witness. Whether Louise complained to her or not, the observant schoolmistress thought all along that the curate's conduct was overly familiar with a servant. For her taste, the clergyman was all too frequently seen going about the halls in his nightshirt. In her words, there was "something particular" going on between the two of them. Nonetheless, under questioning by Mr. Byles, the woman admitted that she had never spoken either with the curate or with the Rev. Mr. Bates about her concerns. Did not the elder woman, having been confided in by a girl of just seventeen, feel a responsibility to do something to protect this innocent housemaid from the "something particular" she thought was going on? Yet she did not reprove Mr. Waldron; she never told Mr. Bates, in fact she told no one. Her bedroom directly adjoined Louisa's, yet she never heard anything? Mrs. Childs, a widow, also admitted that she held the position of village schoolmistress at the discretion of the Rev. Bates and was directly answerable to him. He could dismiss her at any time.

Mr. Thomas Bates was the rector's brother. He was a solicitor with offices in the family's hometown of Heddon-in-the-Wall, Northumberland and in London. His wife had died suddenly at their London home in Kensington Gore. He had been left with infant children and it was soon clear to him that he was in need of additional staffing for the house. He discussed it with his brother who soon reported back that his departing curate had spoken highly of a young woman – Louisa Johnson. It was not that long after Louisa's arrival in Kensington that it became clear that she was carrying a child. On 6 December, he wrote to his brother: "L.J. has been unwell. I shall send her home. Don't say anything about it. Let her mother find it out; it will soon show itself." When the Rev. Bates wrote back, expressing his suspicions, Thomas replied that, if true, the "scoundrel must go to the dogs, with his victim." He saw no reason why he should change that opinion.

The Rev. Dr. William Bates, at last, clambered into the witness box. He had first welcomed Mr. Waldron to Burnham Market in 1852. He had no reason to complain at all about the curate's performance of his ecclesiastical duties. Traditionally, with larger rectories and vicarages, a curate might find lodging with his employer. As the new Burnham Market rectory was then under construction, he had provided lodgings for the Rev. Waldron at the national school (deducting £8 from the curate's £100 salary). Mr. Waldron was at the rectory for dinner, most every Sunday and often twice a week. Rev. Bates said that he had occasionally wondered about the advisability of Mr. Waldron living in such close proximity of a young female servant. The two men had discussed the issue of the proper servant for a clergyman and Waldron had quipped, "I don't see why I shouldn't have a pretty one." The rector said he began to be concerned about his curate's cavalier views on such affairs. Gossip had even reached his ears that Mr. Waldron had been linked to a married woman in Burnham. At the dinner soon before Waldron's departure for Leicestershire, Bates raised the matter. The rector insisted he made no accusations but told Waldron the subject gave him unease. He recalled that the curate answered him with a laugh: "You are always worrying yourself to death about people's characters. Everybody does the same. I do it, you do it, everybody does it." Bates took that to mean that his curate believed that "everybody fornicates."

The stage was now cleared for the testimony of the Rev. Frederick William Walrond. Questioned by his counsel, Mr. Byles, the schoolmaster swore that he had never had criminal intercourse with Louisa Johnson.

He had never kissed her and nor taken even the slightest liberties with the young woman. He had lived in the same house and on the same floor with the young woman for a little more than a year. Of course, it was normal that they should see each other almost every day. It should not be viewed as being anyway improper for a friendly relationship to have been established. She cleaned his room, did some mending, etc. He was satisfied with her work and had recommended her when told by the rector of the needs of Mr. Thomas Bates for an additional servant. There was no possibility, the clergyman swore, that he was the father of her child.

As for his alleged un-clerical nonchalance about matters of the heart, Mr. Waldron said it was simply not true. They had been discussing a man Waldron described as "a dirty little fellow," and he had simply asked why the rector would worry about such a man. He could not ever recall using the expression, "Everybody does it." In fact, the first time he had ever heard the phrase was when the rector used it during his earlier testimony. There had been no problems in his relationship with Mr. Bates until their disagreement over his request for additional money for handling the heavier workload in the rector's six-week absence. In fact, the great bulk of the table talk he remembered from his last dinner in Burnham Market had to do with money matters.

The former curate was now handed off to the rector's counsel, Mr. Prendergast. He would bid to make it clear that Mr. Waldron was a more than unconventional clergyman. Why had the witness left the navy, Prendergast inquired? Waldron said he left rather than face a court-martial for refusing to obey an order that he had thought was unlawful. He admitted getting into an altercation in Burnham Market with Frederick Priest, a churchwarden and the surgeon at the local workhouse. He regretted it. He acknowledged that he had developed a close friendship with Mrs. Priest. It was nothing more than that. He admitted writing a letter to her asking that she find out more about the "stinking medicines" Dr. Priest was making up for the Rev. Mr. Bates. Waldron had suggested to Mrs. Priest that the rector was carrying on with one of his servants, "Who in Burnham does not believe he is living in abominable sin?" In his letter, he told Mrs. Priest it was now "War to the knife and I know enough to shut him up for life!" Waldron said he did not feel it was an inappropriate letter for a gentleman to write to another man's wife. Lastly, Waldron again denied that he had ever suggested that "everybody does it," in the sense that everyone has a lover. He could not recall ever having said that fornication was nothing more than a venial sin. When pressed, however, Mr. Waldron conceded that he might have said something to the effect that there are many worse sins than fornication and "I say so still."

Returning his line of questioning from the theoretical rules of love-making to the actual, Prendergast asked why Waldron had ignored Louisa's repeated letters. If her story was untrue and she was attempting to extort money from him, as he had claimed, why had he not gone to the police? He said he thought her letters were "artful." They amused him. To have replied to her, Waldron said, would have been to enter into a line of communication he had no wish to begin.

The short list of additional witnesses for Mr. Waldron included a Mrs. Mitchell. She took in the laundry and linens from the teacher's household and testified that she had regularly dealt with the sheets from Louisa Johnson's bedroom. The sheets, the jury was informed in as discreetly roundabout way as possible, showed no evidence of a man having been present.

The last witness was Louisa's friend Polly Grix. The young lady was also in service in Burnham Market. Polly testified that Louisa had once told her that she had taken quite a fancy for the cart-maker's apprentice, Norris. He had returned the admiration, having given her a pincushion and a needle book he had purchased at a fair. Polly also said that she had seen Louisa and Norris walking out after dark.

Mr. Prendergast, in his questions for Polly Grix, suggested that the witness had quite exaggerated a simple village flirtation. Prendergast suggested that, if Polly were out walking with them, how could Louisa and Norris have had the privacy to commit the act suggested by her testimony? Had she ever seen them kissing or holding hands? Polly said she had not. Prendergast then asked if Polly was at all familiar with Mr. Waldron. The cheerful lass said she was indeed and added that he had asked her to come to Leicestershire as his servant. He had been very nice to her. Once he even let her sit on his knee and kissed her but it was only "by way of a joke."

Understandably discomfited by this damaging admission by one of his own witnesses, Mr. Byles begged the court to be allowed to recall the Rev. Waldron to contradict the evidence just heard. The curate was re-sworn to state in a loud voice, "I never kissed Mary Ann (Polly) Grix or ever had her on my knee." From the bench, however, the Chief Baron leaned in to intone, "But she says you did." Not for nothing was it said of Lord Pollock, "He belonged to that class of judges who distinctly take a side in the course of a case and makes no mystery to the jury of the opinion which they have formed."

In his closing argument, Prendergast naturally made capital from Polly Grix's surprising admission, suggesting it was additional evidence for the jury of Mr. Waldron's penchant for skirt-chasing. Of course, the larger and more serious charge involved the seduction of Louisa Johnson. The question for the jury was not really whether or not Rev. Waldron was the father of Louisa's child. Louisa swore that it was so, but she was not the defendant on trial for libel. The counsel for Mr. Bates explained that the evidence had shown that the rector had every reason to believe that his curate was responsible for that young woman's fall. The curate's conduct toward Louisa, a young woman who shared his intimate quarters, was certainly inappropriate. His expressed views on fornication could only be described as extremely lax for a clergyman. The jurors must agree that Mr. Bates surely had reason to accept the housemaid's story as true, and therefore, he had no less than a public duty to communicate that belief to the trustees of the Sedley School.

On behalf of the Rev. Waldron, Byles painted his client as a victim. After a falling out over a few pounds wages, the Rev. Mr. Bates had developed a strong bias against his curate. Now after many impoverished years as a curate, Waldron had won a lucrative and valued appointment as a schoolmaster, where he had begun his duties, receiving high marks from his employers. After he had left Burnham Market behind, a former servant begins writing him letters demanding money, insisting he is the father of her child? Of course, in 1855, there could be no proof of paternity. If Miss Johnson was annoyed by the curate's attentions, why did she not report him to the rector? She admits to "sewing" in his room and being taken onto his knee. Was she as innocent as the other side wished the jury to believe? If she was of the type of young woman to sit on a gentleman's knee, how can anyone be certain that she did not have other suitors? Would the Rev. Mr. Waldron, knowing that he had debauched this young woman, have then sent her off to be a servant for the brother of a man he now considered his enemy? As for the Rev. Bates, the accuser was a man quick to pick a fight. After years as a fellow at a great Cambridge institution, he was presented with a church under its patronage. It was a strange act of gratitude for him to almost immediately sue the College. In Burnham Market, the rector was ever ready to cast aspersions at the moral behaviour of his own parishioners. Did he see "fornicators" everywhere? He had sent Mr. Waldron off to the school with a glowing recommendation, yet he quickly accepted the word of a servant girl against him. He did not even interview the accusing woman before writing to Mr. Needham at Sedley. Would not a reasonable man have approached Mr. Waldron first for an explanation before writing such a letter claiming to have "irrefragable proof?" Where was the proof? As for the last minute admission from Polly Grix, she was but a "mere girl" and could not be credited. The Rev. Waldron's career and prospects had been ruined and he was due compensation for the malicious scandal cast upon him by the rector of Burnham Market.

The Chief Baron instructed the jury at some length. The letters from Louisa to her supposed lover were of great interest to Lord Pollock. A truly innocent man would have immediately replied to deny the charge and denounce his accuser. While it is true that Louisa did not mention her pregnancy in her first letter, the Chief Baron suggested that a young woman of seventeen might not be as readily aware of approaching maternity. If they believed the girl, Mr. Waldron's suit must fail. If they believed Mr. Waldron, they must consider whether Mr. Bates had acted maliciously, driven by the alarming bitterness that had grown up between the two men. The Norfolk jurymen were out for just two hours before returning with their verdict that they believed that the Rev. Dr. Bates was not guilty of libel.

Though Mr. Bates left the courtroom the putative winner and Mr. Waldron slunk away in disgrace, the proceedings had been an embarrassment to the church and, regardless of the outcome, had hardly been edifying for either gentleman. *The Norwich Mercury* delivered a typical comment:

> Those, whose life has afforded them a tolerable experience, never, perhaps, remember an action which, while its proceedings excited indignation, carried with it greater exposure, or so great an interest … There was something rotten in the state of Burnham. Rector and curate have struggled to destroy each other; and in which contest, whatever the verdict, the wounds inflicted upon both must be deep and almost unrecoverable.

For the Rev. Mr. Waldron, the earlier expressed level of support from the trustees notwithstanding, he could not retain his position. He left the Sedley School. Traces of his presence can be found in the census reports. In 1861, he married Isabella Drew in Croydon. In 1871, he, his wife and a daughter, were living in Woolwich where he was listed as a tutor. He remained a clergyman, although he does not appear in Crockford's Clerical Directory until 1872, when he was very briefly the rector of Begbrook in Oxfordshire. He died that same year at the age of 51.

The Rev. Mr. Bates continued to serve as rector of Burnham Market for another two decades until his death in 1878. He remained single until rather late in life. In April 1869, at the elevated age of 58, he married Hannah Orford of Ipswich. It is very unlikely that the subject of fornication came up again at the rectory dinner table.